# ATHENE Series

General Editors

**Gloria Bowles**
**Renate Klein**
**Janice Raymond**

Consulting Editor

**Dale Spender**

The Athene Series assumes that all those who are concerned with formulating explanations of the way the world works need to know and appreciate the significance of basic feminist principles.

The growth of feminist research internationally has called into question almost all aspects of social organization in our culture. The Athene Series focuses on the construction of knowledge and the exclusion of women from the process—both as theorists and subjects of study—and offers innovative studies that challenge established theories and research.

ATHENE, the Olympian goddess of wisdom, was honored by the ancient Greeks as the patron of arts and sciences and guardian of cities. She represented both peace and the intellectual aspect of war. Her mother, Metis, was a Titan and presided over all knowledge. While pregnant with Athene, Metis was swallowed whole by Zeus. Some say this was his attempt to embody her supreme wisdom. The original Athene is thus twice born: once of her strong mother, Metis, and once more out of the head of Zeus. According to feminist myth, there is a "third birth" of Athene when she stops being an agent and mouthpiece of Zeus and male dominance, and returns to her original source: the wisdom of womankind.

# *FATHER* KNOWS BEST

## The Use and Abuse
## of *POWER* in
## Freud's Case of *DORA*

**Robin Tolmach Lakoff**
**James C. Coyne**

TEACHERS COLLEGE PRESS
Teachers College, Columbia University
New York and London

Published by Teachers College Press, 1234 Amsterdam Avenue
New York, New York 10027

Excerpt from "Fragment of an Analysis of a Case of Hysteria" from *The Collected
Papers of Sigmund Freud, Volume III*, Authorized translation by Alix and James
Strachey. Published by Basic Books, Inc. 1959 by arrangement with the Hogarth Press
Ltd. and the Institute of Psycho-Analysis, London. Reprinted by permission of Basic
Books, a division of HarperCollins Publishers, Inc. Permission for use of the fragment
in publication outside the U.S. granted by Random Century Group, London.

*Library of Congress Cataloging-in-Publication Data*

Lakoff, Robin Tolmach.
    Father knows best : the use and abuse of power in Freud's case of
Dora / Robin Tolmach Lakoff, James C. Coyne.
        p.    cm.—(Athene series ; 36)
    Includes bibliographical references and index.
    ISBN 0-8077-6267-9 (alk. paper).—ISBN 0-8077-6266-0 (pbk. :
alk. paper)
        1. Hysteria—Case studies.   2. Psychoanalysis—Case studies.
3. Language and languages—Political aspects—Case studies.
4. Sexism in language—Case studies.   5. Women and psychoanalysis—
Case studies.   6. Freud, Sigmund, 1856–1939—Language.   7. Bauer,
Ida, 1882–1945—Mental health.   I. Coyne, James C., 1947–.
II. Title.   III. Series.
RC532.L35   1993
616.89'17'082—dc20                                            92-23887

ISBN 0-8077-6267-9
ISBN 0-8077-6266-0 (pbk.)

Printed on acid-free paper

Manufactured in the United States of America

99  98  97  96  95  94  93        8  7  6  5  4  3  2  1

# Contents

Preface ................................................. vii

1     The Lasting Significance of *Dora* ................... 1

2     The Case History Summarized ...................... 15

3     Previous Discussion of *Dora* ........................ 22

4     Some Linguistic Background ........................ 43

5     Language in the Therapeutic Interaction ......... 60

6     Communication in *Dora* ............................. 77

7     The Interpersonal Framework:
      An Alternative Model .................................. 99

8     Dora as Female Patient ............................... 111

9     Summary and Conclusions ........................... 132

References ........................................... 137

Index .................................................. 143

About the Authors ................................ 151

# Preface

This book had its genesis over 10 years ago in conversations between the authors (then both at Berkeley) about Freud's management of Dora's therapy and how that therapy might have been undertaken differently today. Over time, the discussions evolved into an article, then a long article; from there it metamorphosed into a monograph, and finally into its current form.

In the years of the work's gestation, the nature of the collaboration itself has been in flux as the interests and other commitments of the two authors have shifted. Additionally, developments within many fields (psychoanalysis and psychotherapy, linguistics, literary criticism, and feminism) have altered and enriched our perspective and encouraged changes in design, focus, and scope. While the 10-year odyssey has at times been frustrating, and while we have sometimes despaired of the results ever seeing the light of day, on the whole the waiting has been valuable to us and, we hope, to the book itself.

To the extent that it is meaningful to assign responsibility to the individual authors for specific parts of the text, James Coyne bears principal responsibility for Chapters 2 and 7, and Robin Lakoff for the rest. But counting pages would be deceptive, since every page of this final version reflects the genesis of the whole, the early discussions, the intermediate production of drafts and exchanging of criticism, and the final editing. The book is, and should be seen as, an amalgam of the views and efforts of both authors working jointly.

Others have made significant contributions to this work, throughout its life. We want especially to thank Gloria Bowles, in her capacities as colleague, friend, and astute critic, as well as one of the General Editors of the Athene Series. She has been a source of encouragement and support even when we doubted publication could ever occur. Her efforts to bring this book to light make her virtually a third collaborator.

We owe a similar debt of gratitude to our editors, Lisa Tantillo, Mary Grace Luke, Sarah Biondello, and Neil Stillman. Their insightful comments have greatly improved the work and caught countless errors; their skillful editing has made publication a reality; their patience and good humor in the face of real-world obstacles have been an inspiration to us.

We are grateful to several friends and colleagues whose comments and discussion, over the years, have been most helpful to us. Frederic C. Crews and Doris Treisman read earlier versions and made valuable comments. Anonymous readers have also contributed to our understanding. Finally, we thank friends whose intellectual and moral support have sustained us and taught us a great deal: Mandy Aftel and Elizabeth Krainer. All errors and infelicities remain, of course, our own responsibility.

# 1

# The Lasting Significance of *Dora*

In 1900 Sigmund Freud undertook, at her father's request, the analysis of an 18-year-old woman to whom he gave the pseudonym "Dora." Her symptoms included a (probably not serious) suicidal gesture and *petite hystérie*: a cough, loss of voice, stomach ailments, and a sense of malaise, among other minor symptoms. After 3 months of treatment, Dora abruptly and without explanation broke off the analysis. Since that time, psychoanalysts beginning with Freud himself have sought the reason for its failure and wondered whether that failure might have been foreseen and prevented. Freud wrote up his recollections of the case shortly afterward and, after keeping them for some 4 years in his desk drawer, published them in 1905 as *Fragment of an Analysis of a Case of Hysteria* (which we shall refer to hereafter as *Dora*).

Over the century since it was written, *Dora* has inspired a veritable deluge of commentary and critique, from a great variety of fields. Within psychoanalysis, both the orthodoxy and schismatics as diverse as Jacques Lacan (1966) and Jeffrey Masson (1988) have commented on it; beyond, it has been pored over by literary critics, Marxists, and feminists, among others. While interest in orthodox psychoanalysis may be said to have waned in recent years, interest in this one case continues, as witnessed by the publication a few years back of a collection of significant articles on the topic (Bernheimer & Kahane, 1985). More remarkably, the last several years have seen the production of a movie and a play about Dora. Most recently, Decker (1990) has illuminated the case by setting it in its social and historical context. The fascination seems insatiable.

And now, this investigation is added to the clutter. A reader might properly ask, Why? If, indeed, the case is nearly a century old; if the theoretical flaws that haunted Dora's analysis have (it is claimed) been remedied; if psychoanalysis itself is in retreat; and if so very much about the case already exists . . . , why stir up the ashes once again? Is there anything left to be said about Dora, or *Dora*, or Freud and Dora? And if there is, does anyone care to hear it?

Our argument for disinterring *Dora* yet once more is this: We are not so much interested (as an analyst might be) in criticizing the interaction between Freud and his patient as an exemplar of analytic procedure; nor are we principally concerned with the case as an instance of therapeutic interpretive technique or as an illustration of hermeneutic method or theory, although both of these focuses certainly are relevant to ours, as underpinnings.

We see the case, Freud's representation of it, and its consequences as we know them, as raising troubling questions about the psychotherapeutic relationship in general: in 1900, in 2000; in psychoanalysis and in its more recent evolutions and devolutions. We will argue that, while much of the method Freud exemplified in *Dora* has changed, the basic relation between therapist and client/patient, their power relations and the consequences thereof, remains necessarily and intrinsically unaltered. Any changes that theoretical revision has introduced are, at best, cosmetic with regard to power relations. We suggest, further, that a nonegalitarian power dynamic is unavoidable if therapeutic change is to occur; but that, as a result of its existence, abuse of the less by the more powerful member of the dyad becomes (as illustrated by Freud's treatment of Dora) an omnipresent threat, to be guarded against zealously by both participants (but with the therapist, as the more powerful member, bearing the major responsibility). We suggest that the sorts of abuse that are encountered in therapies of all kinds go far beyond sexual misconduct. Any infringement of a client's or patient's moves toward autonomy is ipso facto abusive. And finally, we suggest that the danger of abuse and the seriousness of the damage it can do are exacerbated if the unavoidable power imbalance of the consulting room underscores a greater discrepancy between therapist and patient/client in the outside world—as is inevitably the case, for instance, if a therapist belongs to a politically dominant group (based on, for instance, race, class, ethnicity, or gender) and the patient/client does not. Gender, as the oldest and greatest source of power discrepancy, is apt to cause the deepest problems—problems

*Dora* demonstrates with painful clarity, but that could as easily occur in a present-day therapeutic relationship. The only difference is that today's analysts are careful to disguise their sexism or conceal it, perhaps even from themselves. So a close examination of *Dora* throws into sharp relief problems that still exist today, shrouded though they may be in politically correct expression. Plus ça change, plus c'est la même chose.

Analysts view *Dora* as paradigmatic: Like Freud's other case histories, and perhaps even more graphically than most, it provides a glimpse through the keyhole of the consulting room, showing how Freud actually carried out analyses. At the same time, its failure provides grist for the theoretical mill: Can the error be identified precisely, and avoided? Is it an error that might still be made? Does the fault lie with doctor or patient—or perhaps in the psychoanalytic method itself? These questions, variously answered over the years, remain of crucial importance in a field in which theoretical correctness can be measured, if at all, only by therapeutic outcome.

The case history also serves as an invaluable resource for the history of psychoanalysis: a memoir of the early days in which Freud searched for solutions to the riddle of the psyche, developing theory and method as he went along. A great deal of what was later solidified as dogma first appears here, explicitly stated or covertly hinted at. It was through this case, for instance, by his own testimony, that Freud came to understand the significance of the transference, and the importance of interpreting it early in an analysis. The monograph has also come to illustrate and legitimize the assumptions and methods of analysis and those forms of intrapsychic therapy derived from it: anamnesis, interpretation, and a strong emphasis on the patient's unconscious, at the expense of real events in her current and interpersonal world. *Dora* serves the field of psychoanalysis as a training manual, a set of instructions and steps to be followed, with its failure the only (admittedly critical) flaw, one easily remedied once it is perceived. "The description of Freud's fragmentary work with Dora," said Erikson (1962, p. 455), "has become the classical analysis of the structure and genesis of hysteria."

Feminists (e.g., Chesler, 1972) take a different view of *Dora*, seeing in it a representation of what is most dangerous to women's autonomy in the psychoanalytic model. It illustrates in gruesome detail the dangers for a woman of submitting her psyche to a therapist, and especially a male therapist, who has unthinkingly

accepted his culture's stereotypes about male and female status in
society and "normal" behavior, and uses his position as a figure of
authority to reinforce those assumptions. Marxist commentators
(e.g., Lichtman, 1982) have seen in the study an unwillingness to
recognize capitalist society's complicity in Dora's dilemma and
have commented on the futility of an attempt to "heal" people
like Dora while leaving their milieu unexamined. Conversely,
schismatic analysts like Jacques Lacan (1966) and his followers[1]
have seen this case as an exemplification of their argument that
the symbolic representations of the unconscious are the basis of
symptomatology such as Dora's—not her milieu at all. Literary
critics (e.g., Marcus, 1975) have seen the case as an opening wedge
for the modern novel: The hint of the unreliable narrator, the
technique of stream-of-consciousness, and other current fictional
devices receive either their origin or impetus from this vivid case
history.

The fact that *Dora* has been studied from so many perspectives offers the advantage of multiply enriching insights, offset by
the liability of confusion and the tendency of investigators in one
field to be unaware of work in others. We have tried here to bring
together and summarize the findings of all relevant fields and
place them in some sort of coherent relation to one another. Additionally, we have brought in still other viewpoints from fields that
have not previously been brought to bear: interpersonal systems
theory and linguistic pragmatics. Not surprisingly, these are fields
that have come into being or achieved full maturity relatively
recently; still less surprisingly, they happen to be our own.

Two overriding questions have been paramount from the beginning of research on *Dora*, and remain unresolved today: the
source and meaning of Dora's symptoms; and the effect of Freud's
intervention. The source of Dora's problems has been identified
in several ways: (1) as purely internal and intrapsychic—the perspective of orthodox psychoanalysis—within which Dora's problems with Herr K are the result of her own "abnormality," her
neurosis; to focus on and make changes in her external environment, in this view, would be only to exacerbate the illness; (2) as
purely external, the perspective of Marxist, and some feminist,
theory, which sees Dora's difficulties as created within her family
because of its social and economic structure and capitalism's need
for such unhealthy relationships. In this perspective, therapy of
any kind is worse than futile: It encourages the patient to blame
herself for her distress, and by turning her criticism inward, to

evade the responsibility to work for social change; (3) as mixed, the perspective of interpersonal systems theory, in which attention is concentrated on the interactional system within which the patient is involved, which in turn is seen as a mediator between the individual psyche and the demands and constraints of the larger society (cf. Coyne, 1985, 1987; Watzlawick, Weakland, & Fisch, 1974; Watzlawick, Beavin, & Jackson, 1967). In this view, the family, exemplifying and enacting the inhumane values of the larger society, inculcates them in the minds of its members, most destructively in the case of the weakest and most dependent. Therapy must not belittle the importance of society's contribution; but "society" cannot be changed quickly or thoroughly enough to bring relief to those who are currently suffering. If the destructive patterns within the structure of the family itself can somehow be reworked or redirected, then suffering can be alleviated; failing that, the therapist may work to empower an individual to act to alter his or her participation in the patterns that are proving self-destructive (Coyne, 1987). Judged by its own standards, each perspective is likely to generate a plausible account of a given patient/client's behavior and of the outcome of treatment, one that is consistent with the evidence that it selects and organizes. When intrapsychic and interpersonal approaches are brought into contrast, disputes can seldom be resolved with references to data alone, but rather become a matter of the aesthetic, practical, or ethical prejudices of the particular therapist or investigator.

In embarking on a critique of the effects of psychoanalysis on this young woman (especially if we are to contrast it with other possible approaches), it is important to realize that Dora was the kind of patient for whom psychoanalytic therapy had been devised, and with whom, consequently, it might be particularly expected to succeed. She was young, intelligent, and articulate,[2] and living with her family, who were sympathetic to Freud's work. It is true that she entered analysis not of her own free will but at her father's behest, but she was both emotionally and economically dependent on him, and therefore well-motivated, at least at the start, toward success. The diagnosis was *petite hystérie*, the condition most amenable to analytic intervention; the symptoms were not serious enough to be life threatening, nor had most of them been in existence very long. In short, Dora was Freud's ideal patient, according to his own explicit standards.

Therefore, his failure must have been particularly disappointing and humiliating to Freud (encouraging, no doubt, his insistence that Dora had broken off the treatment for revenge). Hence it is important for the prestige and self-respect of the analytic movement that this failure should be explicable on grounds that do not call into question the philosophy, theory, or method of psychoanalysis itself. So it is not surprising that, since the original publication of this case, there have been many attempts from within the profession to explain what went wrong; nor is it remarkable that their conclusions do not differ significantly from one another, and that these writers have failed to call for a reexamination of Freud's basic and unexamined premise: that psychoanalytic therapy is the treatment of choice for someone in Dora's situation.

It is even less remarkable that these writers (and, indeed, most commentators on *Dora* from most fields) have failed to examine the basic questions that Freud's failure with Dora raises: Is psychoanalysis (as opposed to other forms of psychotherapy) *ever* the method of choice? Is psychotherapy (in general) appropriate or helpful in cases like Dora's in which the outside world contributes heavily to the problems? Is psychoanalysis even properly considered a *method*, in the sense of being coherent and rigorous, with predictable relations between therapist's actions and effects on patients?

From this perspective, *Dora* is best read as a cautionary tale about the use and abuse of power in present-day psychotherapy. No current analytic theoretical or methodological assumptions can prevent the recurrence of the tragedy of *Dora*. Understanding, and interpretation, of the transference—or the countertransference, or indeed anything belonging strictly to either participant's intrapsychic sphere—cannot keep the error from being repeated, because its source is not there. (We are not saying that these concepts have no utility; only that for the kinds of problems that plagued Freud and Dora, they are of little avail.) The assumption that analysts, by virtue of their position as well as the job they do, are both required and entitled to hold an inordinate amount of power over their analysands requires close examination—which will reveal it to be seriously flawed. Too often the medical analogy that Freud was fond of is used, without deeper inspection, to suggest that like physicians, analysts must and do hold over their patients a power both essential and benign. This may have been an acceptable assumption at the turn of the century, but now we see the damage that arises from that unexamined belief. In the first place, the analyst, *qua* analyst, is not a medical doctor: Freud himself, in *The Question of Lay Analysis* (1926/1959), made it clear that the analyst's work was quite distinct from that of the physician. (His frequent metaphorical conflation of the two roles makes sense only if read as not implying a literal equation.) And secondly and more importantly, we know that even physicians are not infallible, and competent patients must accept responsibility for their medical care, sharing power that formerly was the doctor's alone.

Another argument might be made against bringing the problems between Freud and his early patient into the current therapeutic context: that psychoanalysis has learned so much, and changed so much, since 1900 that the dangers of *Dora* are confined to the Viennese past and could never happen here or now. If modifications in the understanding of the psyche could circumvent the disaster of Dora's analysis (as most analytic commentators have supposed), this comment would be valid. The response of the analytic community to the criticisms of Jeffrey Masson, based in part on points similar to those we are making, suggests that it is not and has never been prepared for searching self-examination, and still less for the changes in theory and technique that would naturally arise as a result. Cavalier dismissal of feminist criticism of analytic theory from within the profession (cf. the diatribe of Eissler, 1977) shows that this criticism has been neither integrated into current analytic thinking nor fully understood. Superficial acceptance into the theory of feminist critique has much the same effect. Arguments that the profession has matured so as to change radically its view of women, and its members' treatment of women, must somehow account for comments like those of Lewin (1974):

> One could well imagine such a girl [as Dora] leading men on, frustrating them, and finally destroying them altogether. . . . Hell hath no fury like a woman scorned. (521–522)

It is true that Lewin made these remarks before modern feminism had its full effect on psychoanalysis; but it seems improbable that the ingrained androcentrism of the passage cited could be wiped out of the minds of analysts within a single generation. What they may *say* in their writings, or to their patients, is less significant than what they were taught to believe by their own analysts or read in the writings of Freud and other revered progenitors, and still, deep in their hearts believe.

While late-twentieth-century therapists may indeed have di-
vested themselves of the more overt and embarrassing sexist assumptions of their forebears—especially in the interpretive, or
semantic, area (e.g., penis envy or female masochism)—in the
relation between client/patient and therapist (that is, pragmatically), assumptions justifying and justified by the ancient relationship between the sexes continue to flourish. Especially when the
therapist is male and the patient/client female, the two sources
of power imbalance function synergistically to cause a serious
potential for abuse, that is, the denial of the patient or client's
autonomy.

We have discussed these issues at length in informal conversations as well as formal presentations to members of the therapeutic community, over several years. Entirely too often, when we
bring up the power imbalance, we hit an impasse: Therapists (especially orthodox analysts) simply refuse to believe that any such
situation exists. Nor are these responses dispassionate. Rather,
they are expressed with anger and pain—emotions that are inappropriate to the circumstances.

What is to be made of these reactions? We suspect that our
interlocutors sometimes simply don't understand what we're saying, but are unwilling to take the trouble to move beyond a gut
reaction. It's true that "power" and "inequality" are fighting
words in current American discourse. But since we agree that
therapeutic discourse *must* be nonegalitarian if it is to be effective,
our use of the term is not intended to convey a value judgment.
But if inequality is ignored or denied, the abuse that it can engender cannot be acknowledged, much less diagnosed or cured. To
refuse to acknowledge the way in which therapy necessarily operates at its best is to be unable to deal with it at its worst.

In other ways the profession diverts or deflects needed critique, rather than growing by confronting it intelligently. Too
often, Freud's claims, theoretical and methodological, have been
shielded from criticism by the argument that, unpleasant as they
are, they represent scientific thinking. So the biological reality of
the Oedipus complex, with its inevitable concomitants, women's
lesser morality and lower intelligence and creativity, departs from
its origins as speculation or hypothesis—a poetic leap rather than a
scientific conclusion—to become a biologically unalterable cross-
cultural human universal. Too easily overlooked is the fact that
the "evidence" for the scientific claims consists only of the inter-

pretations of a not disinterested investigator, firmly fixed in his own time and place. Science, then, becomes just another repressive device. As phrenology and its allied pseudo-sciences were used in the nineteenth century to justify the oppression and mistreatment of non-Aryans in more than one Western country, so psychoanalytic "findings" were (and are) used to legitimize misogyny and the continued repression of women. Worse, women, as analysts or patients, were bullied into becoming advocates for their detractors' methods. It was a classic double bind. If women agreed with psychoanalysis that they were stupider, weaker, and less moral than men, then at least those individuals who agreed could be exalted as "honorary men," women who had risen high enough above their baseness to appreciate that baseness. But a woman who was not convinced of the reality of penis envy and its concomitants thereby demonstrated her inability to think rationally and scientifically, as well as her moral corruptibility. Arguments of this sort, however delicately phrased, continue into the present—and need, along with the unexamined presuppositions that continue to fuel them, to be brought to the light of day. We can no longer accept the statement that "this is science" as a valid argument. It has become clear that psychoanalytic "discoveries" seldom deserve the status of scientific constructs. The Oedipus complex does not have the status of the cholera bacillus, or even the charmed quark. And even were it scientifically demonstrable, it would be necessary to prove that all the hypotheses Freud deduced from it had equally validable (or rather, falsifiable) status.

It is argued in response to such criticism that of course psychoanalysis must operate as Freud and his successors stipulate, with inequality and a lack of reciprocity between participants, in order to facilitate the transference; that transference and resistance are the means by which change is necessarily accomplished; and that it is naive to suggest changes in these basic assumptions (even if they could be changed). This argument lacks logical rigor: How do we *know* that transference is the mechanism of change, and if it is, how do we know that the power imbalance is prerequisite to it? Therapies making much less theoretical use of transference report essentially the same levels of "improvement" or "change" as psychoanalysis. But the argument can still be made that, theoretically justified or not, a power imbalance necessarily arises out of the nature of the relationship between a therapist who possesses information and skills and a client who lacks (and comes into therapy to get) them. Further, interpretive therapies require unilateral interpretability, reinforcing the inequality. But the fact that a power imbalance is unavoidable should not seduce us into unconditionally accepting its consequences. Technique, like its theoretical underpinnings, must be continually re-evaluated. What made unquestioned sense in the world of nineteenth-century Vienna, with its rigid social stratifications and hierarchical authority structures, may very well work less efficiently in twenty-first-century America. If psychoanalysis can supplement its traditional techniques with others that circumvent the criticisms that have been leveled at it (or truly demonstrate to the satisfaction of independent observers that these criticisms are invalid), well and good. But if dependence on solely intrapsychic assumptions and authoritarian interventions turns out to be indispensable to the framework, perhaps it is time to ask about the relevance of the theory and method to our times, to ask whether they can be integrated into a therapy that treats its subjects as striving intelligently toward full personhood. (For an example of such an approach see Yalom, 1989.) It should not need remarking, but perhaps does, that an important difference between science and religion is that in the former, no assumption is sacred: Everything can be and must be questioned. In the latter, argumentation serves mainly to buttress the conclusions of the past. Psychoanalysis and its proponents show a disquieting tendency (for an "art-science") to fall into the second type of argumentation: It's always been done this way; Freud tells us to do it this way, so there can't be another way. Until there is evidence (through controlled experiment, a rather improbable occurrence) of a biconditional causal link between orthodox analytic method and psychic change, it is imperative that the field leave itself open to changes in method, making the analytic relationship more like those we encounter in contemporary real life. Decker (1990) suggests that psychoanalytic theory and practice are malleable, changing in response to changing times and mores:

> As the twentieth century draws to a close, the distinctiveness and longevity of adolescence in the West, the partial success of the feminist movement, and the receptivity of psychoanalysts to the idea of personality change throughout life all mean that a teenage girl with Dora's problems will usually encounter analysts and other psychotherapists responsive to the specific concerns of her age. (p. 197)

But while it is undeniable that analytic *theory* has changed to encompass these new ideas, it is less demonstrable that analytic practice, deriving from the attitudes of analysts themselves, has done the same, and Decker's rosy assessment seems more a wish than a demonstrated reality.

While alternative therapeutic models provide a form of critique by comparison and contrast, linguistic pragmatics offers a method of analysis of the discourse itself. It focuses on language as a means of communication, a way of conveying ideas and attitudes, explicitly and implicitly; a way for speakers to accept or dodge responsibility for what they wish to convey to their interlocutors. Even a speaker who has determined to express a particular idea has more than one choice of how to express it: directly or indirectly; politely, neutrally, or rudely; ironically, metaphorically, or plainly—just to list a few items on the menu. It follows then that no utterance is neutral, no choice unmarked. And it follows from that that the choices Freud made in *Dora*, in communicating both to his patient and to his readers, were made for a purpose and had discernible consequences. Some of his choices were based, knowingly or not, on Freud's unexamined presuppositions about his world and his discourse context: Who was he, in relation to his patient? What did it mean to "bring her to reason"? Without examining many of these presuppositions, he rushed headlong into the conversation—with predictable effect.

What is Freud doing when he makes interpretations to Dora? Interpretation is not a value-free activity, not pure semantics, but bound up in pragmatic consequences. What is Freud saying (to himself, to Dora, to posterity) when he alleges that Dora broke off the analysis because the transference was not interpreted? Or because she was homosexual? Both of these statements make hidden implications about motives, particularly Dora's; they are not instances of scientific objectivity, though they are framed as such. Freud's choice of language to and about Dora, as well as about the business of analysis itself, must be subjected to inquiry. The rhetoric is not distinct from the content: It *is* the content.

One pragmatic issue is our own decision about the text itself—a problem created by the fact that *Dora* must be seen by English-speaking readers through the prism of translation, and translation creates a text as much as merely transmitting it. We have based our discussion on the English translation of Freud's monograph by James and Alix Strachey, in Volume VII of the *Standard Edition* (1905/1955). One might object that, in a work that involves so much reference to specific utterances and their implications, it is dangerous to rely on a translation. But in this case, given our intentions and purposes, the danger is more apparent than real. To minimize it, we have made use of Joan Riviere's translation (Rieff, 1963) alongside the Stracheys's. They differ very insignificantly on the points of importance to our discussion. Additionally, we are concerned less with the sort of delicate lexical choices in which a translator's decision is crucial, than with the effect of one sort of speech act rather than another: the function of a question at a particular moment in a discourse, the reasons why an indirect rather than a direct way of communicating something might have been chosen, and with what consequences. As the similarities between the translations attest, these larger and more abstract choices are not significantly affected by competent translation. In other words, we are attempting to analyze the notion of "conversation" between patient and therapist, to see what was unusual about *Dora* in relation to a typical analytic conversation (Freud's and those reported by others) and how any observed anomalies might have contributed to the outcome.

From this perspective, there exist curious discrepancies between *Dora* and Freud's other case histories, both of style and content. What does Freud's departure from his normal style tell us about his state of mind? And what did his style communicate to Dora? Since an analysis is a transaction between two real people, not merely a discussion between a patient and his or her intrapsychic constructs, how does the analyst's mood and personality affect the outcome of a therapeutic relationship?

There are other pragmatic considerations in this sort of work. One is the status and reliability of the "conversation" Freud represents in *Dora*. How literally are we to take it as the text that the two actually produced? We are of course not working with a true transcript (such as, for example, Labov and Fanshel's [1977] treatment of a therapeutic discourse). Freud states that he wrote down notes from memory in the 10-minute interludes between Dora's sessions and the next patient's. But we know that memory is unreliable, and memory of emotionally charged events less reliable than most (cf. Loftus, 1979). So Freud's reconstructions of the discourse fall into a category between transcripts and the invented utterances of novelists or syntacticians. But in this respect they are not unlike reports of conversations, in waking life and in dreams, by analysands in their sessions; and analysts have never suggested discarding these as inaccurate and therefore unusable.

As other commentators on this text have implicitly done, we take Freud's reconstructions as essentially accurate—catching at least the spirit of the conversation, a question for a question, a challenge for a challenge. Certainly it would be hard to argue that Freud falsified the conversation to his own advantage, since he hardly comes off well; nor would it make sense (or be characteristic of what we know about Freud) to suppose he falsified it to make himself look worse. So we can take Freud's record as an accurate statement of Freud's and Dora's interactions with each other: perhaps not word for word, but surely intention for intention.

Finally, we should make it explicit that our discussion of interpretation and interpretability embodies a different perspective from much recent discussion of "hermeneutics" (cf., for example, Habermas, 1971; Ricoeur, 1981). Within psychoanalysis and several other fields, there has developed in the last several years a rich literature in this area, essentially focusing on the nature of interpretation: what an interpretation is, when it can be made, how it can be tested and falsified (cf. Schafer, 1976, 1983). This is a semantic issue, and of course one of great importance to psychoanalytic work. We are, however, not viewing interpretation as an artifact in its own right at all, but rather seeing it as a form of interpersonal negotiation, a means by which power is allocated and utilized. We are primarily concerned with the pragmatics of interpretation and interpretability, and for this reason have less to say about its semantic aspect.

These, then, are the major arguments to be made in subsequent chapters:

1. The therapeutic relationship necessarily imposes on its participants an imbalance of power.
2. This imbalance facilitates the development of an abusive relationship, often difficult to discern and to deal with.
3. In case the therapist is male and the client female, the potential for abuse via imbalance of power is greater and more dangerous.
4. The use of interpretation of one member by the other both facilitates and exacerbates the power difference.
5. While *Dora* represents an especially clear and disturbing instance of psychotherapeutic abuse, it is not alone; and the problems it demonstrates are not those of Freud's method in 1900, or orthodox psychoanalysis in 1990, but of *any* thera-

peutic procedure in which unilateral interpretation plays a significant role, and in which one participant is defined as more knowledgeable, healthy, and competent than the other.

In spite of our critique of therapeutic theory and method, both authors recognize the value and validity of competently and sensitively done psychotherapy, if not necessarily orthodox analysis. We argue that the circumvention of therapy's abusive potential is problematic, but certainly possible. Therefore, we do not place ourselves in the antitherapy movement currently spearheaded by Masson (1988). We see ourselves as reformers, not "abolitionists." To us, the institution has proved its intrinsic worth, but can be strengthened by self-examination and restructuring—just like its clients.

## NOTES

1. Discussion of *Dora* by Lacanians may be found in many places. In particular, an issue of *Revue Française de Psychanalyse* (Vol. 37, No. 3, 1973) is devoted to the topic. Bernheimer and Kahane (1985) provide an excellent bibliography of these and other writings on *Dora* up to that time.

2. In other words, Dora closely approximates the ideal female patient identified by Schofield (1964) as the YAVIS (young, attractive, verbally fluent, intelligent, and successful).

# 2

# The Case History Summarized

In his case history, Freud tells Dora's story with an emphasis on the historical events that he saw as contributory to her current psychological state. Here we summarize the same story, slightly changing the perspective to accentuate the interpersonal situation in which the young woman found herself for a number of years. While Freud himself comments on all that we shall report below (there is, after all, no other way to arrive at this information), we have at various points changed his emphasis. It may be helpful for the reader to superimpose one narrative on the other, both for the fullest view of Dora's situation, and because the comparison affords a glimpse of the way two very different therapeutic models would see Dora's history.

Eighteen-year-old Dora lived with her parents and a brother one-and-a-half years her senior. Freud was well-acquainted with her father and thought highly of him. He had never met Dora's mother. Our picture of the family situation is based on the reports that Freud obtained from Dora and her father. There is some indication that the brother would have painted a picture more sympathetic to the mother.

According to Freud, the father was dominating and intelligent, "a man of rather unusual activity and talents" (p. 18).[1] In contrast, the mother is pictured as a foolish and uncultivated woman suffering from what Freud terms "housewife's psychosis." "She had no understanding of her children's more active interests, and was occupied all day long in cleaning the house with its furniture and utensils—to such an extent as to make it almost impossible to use or enjoy them" (p. 20).

Two interwoven sets of circumstances are critical in under-

15

standing the patterning of family relationships: the changes in routine required by the father's real and feigned illnesses and Dora's ties to the K family. Freud's account of the father's illnesses begins with his tuberculosis when Dora was 6 years old. Although his condition quickly improved, as a precaution against further attacks the family moved to a town with a better climate, where they lived for 10 years. The family also spent some of their summers at a health resort. Furthermore, throughout Dora's childhood and adolescence, her father would from time to time cough and complain about the rawness of the climate, and this would be the excuse for him to move to another area, with or more generally without the rest of the family.

When Dora was 10 years old, her father's vision became permanently impaired because of a detached retina, requiring treatment in a darkened room. Although the details are not given, it appears that Dora helped care for him during this period. At the time, Dora overheard her aunt tell her mother that the eye problem was the result of a sexually transmitted disease. More symptoms appeared 2 years later. Following a period of mental confusion, the father showed some paralysis and further mental disturbance. At the urging of a friend, Herr K (who also knew Freud), the father went to Vienna where Freud (in his capacity as a neurologist) prescribed treatment. Apparently the father had contracted syphilis before his marriage and had given it to his wife. When Dora's mother became symptomatic and required treatment, Dora "identified herself with her mother by means of slight symptoms and peculiarities of manner, which gave her an opportunity for some really remarkable achievements in the direction of intolerable behavior" (p. 75). Dora believed that she also had acquired the disease, and she was vocal in her accusations against her father for being the cause of her various physical complaints.

When Dora's family first moved to another town because of the father's tuberculosis, they became acquainted with the K family, who had lived there for a number of years. Frau K, who herself had spent months in a sanatorium for "nervous disorders," nursed Dora's father while her mother stayed out of the sickroom. Although she previously had been unable to walk, Frau K now became a "healthy and lively woman" (p. 33). Dora was close to the Ks, took care of their children, and received presents from Herr K. It was clear to the young Dora that the Ks were having marital problems.

Dora confided in Frau K and discussed sexual matters with her. Together they read books on the physiology of sex. The adolescent became the older woman's "confidante and advisor in all the difficulties in her married life" (p. 61). When Dora stayed at the Ks's home, she shared a bedroom with Frau K (whose husband would sleep elsewhere). Dora was aware that the Ks had discussed divorce. Frau K at first refused to consider a divorce on account of the children; when she later changed her mind, Herr K no longer wanted one. Dora had also observed that Frau K seemed perfectly healthy when her husband was away on business trips, but would become ill again immediately upon his return, thereby avoiding sexual relations.

After the father's recovery, it became apparent that he and Frau K were having an affair. While the families shared a suite of rooms at the health resort, the two gave up their usual bedrooms and moved into new ones that allowed them privacy and freedom from interruption. Dora complained to both her parents, but her mother reassured her that Frau K had saved her father from suicide for the sake of his family, and that therefore the two had a right to be together as they wished. After their return from the resort, Dora's father and Frau K met daily while Herr K was at work. The father gave Frau K money, and, in order to make his "handsome presents" to her less conspicuous, had also begun to give Dora and her mother presents. Dora noticed that the choice of presents reflected Frau K's tastes, and in particular saw that jewelry that her father gave her was identical to some belonging to Frau K that Dora had admired in her presence. Everyone pointedly questioned Frau K about the matter, and Herr K complained bitterly to Dora's mother.

After Dora's family moved from the town in which the Ks lived, her father would complain of deteriorating health, return to the town, and write letters to the family indicating that his health was improving. Dora's family's move to Vienna was soon followed by the arrival of the K family, and Dora regularly saw her father and Frau K together on the street. When Dora's father again complained of bad health and left Vienna, Dora was able to discover that Frau K had also left, on the pretext of visiting relatives.

According to Freud, Dora initially had dismissed signs of the nature of her father's relationship with Frau K and had been an accomplice in the affair: She avoided the Ks's house when she believed her father was there, instead going to meet the children who had been sent outside. Dora resisted a governess' suggestion that there was an affair going on and accused the governess in turn of an interest in her father.

The governess had complained to both Dora and her mother about the affair and had argued to the mother that it was below her dignity to tolerate it. Dora found good reason to doubt the woman's objectivity. When Dora's father was in town, the governess took an active interest in Dora, encouraged her in her studies, and was "ready with every sort of assistance" (p. 37). But when the father was away, the governess was indifferent to her. When she perceived this pattern, Dora became hostile to the governess, made the accusation about her motives, and insisted on her dismissal.

Just as the relationships of the two families were intertwined in complicated ways, so Dora's relationship as an individual with both Frau and Herr K was intricate. Frau K confided in her and initiated her into the mysteries of sex (through talk and reading); Dora babysat for the Ks's small children. From early in the families' relationship, Dora and Herr K spent a great deal of time alone together, and Herr K frequently brought her gifts. When Dora was 14, Herr K enticed her to his office in the city with the promise of watching a church festival. His wife was supposed to be there as well, but unbeknownst to Dora, he had asked his wife to stay away. When Dora arrived, Herr K was alone in the darkened room, the shades drawn. "He then," reports Freud, "came back . . . and suddenly clasped the girl to him and pressed a kiss upon her lips" (p. 28). Dora kept the incident secret.

During Dora's fifteenth year, she received flowers from Herr K every day that he was in the neighborhood, as well as frequent valuable presents. He spent a good deal of his spare time with her. As Freud notes, Dora's parents were well aware of the attention Herr K was showing their daughter, but gave no indication that they regarded it as in any way inappropriate. Freud states that it was advantageous for Dora's father to adopt a benign interpretation of Herr K's behavior.

When she was 16, Dora was staying with the Ks at their house by a lake. One day, while she was walking around the lake, Herr K "had the audacity to make a proposal," the exact content of which is never revealed to us by Freud. He does report, however, that as part of his pleading with Dora, Herr K stated, "You know I get nothing out of my wife" (p. 106). Dora had been told by the Ks's governess that Herr K had similarly approached her, but that after she yielded to him, he lost interest in her. Dora did not allow Herr K to finish the "proposal," but slapped him and ran away.

Dora reported the incident to her mother, but when her father confronted him, Herr K denied making advances to Dora. He accused her of imagining the scene, spoke disparagingly of her, and revealed that he knew from Frau K that Dora had been reading books about sex. Such matters, he argued, had overexcited her, leading her to fantasize the incident. The father accepted his friend's explanation and reproached his daughter.

Freud draws a parallel between Frau K's betrayal of Dora and what happened between Dora's father and her governess. "Frau K had not loved her for her own sake, but on account of her father. Frau K had sacrificed her without a moment's hesitation so that her relations with her father might not be disturbed" (p. 62).

Freud notes that despite this Dora did not become angry with Frau K. Her animosity was directed to her father, whom she accused of handing her over to Herr K to compensate for the affair with his wife. She demanded that her father break off all relations with the K family, but, as he told Freud,

> . . . to begin with, I myself believe that Dora's tale of the man's immoral suggestions is a phantasy that has forced its way into her mind; and besides, I am bound to Frau K by ties of honourable friendship and I do not wish to cause her pain. (p. 20)

Freud does not believe that a formal agreement existed between Herr K and Dora's father, but acknowledges that each of the two men avoided making inferences about the other that would interfere with his own plans. Freud notes that the father seemed to dismiss the possibility of danger in his daughter's spending so much time in the companionship of a man who got "no satisfaction from his wife." Further,

> It was possible for Herr K to send Dora flowers every day for a whole year while he was in the neighbourhood, to take every opportunity of giving her valuable presents, and to spend his spare time in her company, without her parents noticing anything in his behavior that was characteristic of love-making. (p. 35)

From Freud's account, it is difficult to reconstruct the extent to which Dora encouraged Herr K. She rejected Freud's interpretation that she had been in love with him. Yet she did volunteer that one of her cousins had told her, "Why, you're simply wild about that man!" (p. 37). However she may have felt about Herr K, her knowledge that in his proposition to her he was approaching her exactly as he had a servant probably caused considerable anger.

One source of difficulty in understanding Dora's role lies in Freud's contradictory descriptions of her. As Marcus (1975) has noted, Freud refers to her variously as a "girl" and a "child," but treats her throughout as if she has the maturity and capacity for sexual response of a woman.

Dora had suffered for some time from shortness of breath, migraine headaches, a nervous cough, and loss of voice, but these symptoms did not in themselves bring her into therapy. Shortly before the consultation with Freud that initiated her treatment, her parents had found a suicide note that she had written. Freud agreed with her father's judgment that she had no serious suicidal intentions, but the note legitimized the father's bringing her in and served to identify her as "sick." The actual precipitating event was an argument with her father that culminated in her fainting—an argument in which Dora insisted that her father break off his relationship with Herr K, whom she accused of propositioning her, and Frau K, with whom Dora believed he was having an affair. Dora's father pressed Freud to "please try and bring her to reason" (p. 26). He hoped that Freud would convince her that the incident with Herr K was only imaginary, so that she would drop her demands and he could continue his relationship with Frau K undisturbed.

When Dora broke off the analysis, some of her symptoms had been improved, but the basic hysteria remained. Freud saw her once more, briefly, 15 months after the termination of treatment. Shortly after she had broken it off, she told Freud, her symptoms had greatly improved. Thereafter, she visited the Ks, confronting each of them separately with her knowledge, which they did not deny. She had not seen them since. After that, other hysterical symptoms, new and old, had emerged. Freud ended his report on a hopeful note—he understood that Dora had married and "had been reclaimed once more by the realities of life" (p. 122).

But the truth may be less pleasant. We have a report from Felix Deutsch (1957) in evidence. Dora came to him (he was an internist and the husband of the analyst Helene Deutsch) in middle age. From the history she gave him he recognized Freud's famous if pseudonymous patient. She acknowledged the identification. In the intervening years she had, indeed, married (though not the man Freud had assumed) and had two sons, both now adult. But she had not overcome her hysteria. She came to Deutsch for the treatment of severe emphysema (she had become a chain smoker; we may recall that Freud, Dora's father, and Herr K were all "passionate smokers"). She was miserable in her marriage and motherhood, so mistrustful of all the men in her life that she and everyone in her environment were miserable. Deutsch quotes noncommittally a colleague's assessment of Dora as "the most repulsive hysteric I have ever seen."

Above we have sketched the basic case history, deviating very little from Freud's own presentation. In subsequent chapters we will discuss in more detail other perspectives on the case, the relative importance in Dora's symptomatology and subsequent history of the intrapsychic traumas of her earlier life, and the difficulties inherent in her current real-world milieu; we will also discuss certain interesting and troublesome aspects of her fragmentary analysis itself, as reported by Freud. First, however, let us summarize the more relevant items in the flood of literature that has adumbrated the case over the past 80 years.

## NOTE

1. This and all subsequent page numbers not preceded by a date refer to Freud, 1905/1953.

# 3

# Previous Discussion of *Dora*

As a paradigmatic example for psychoanalytic theory and practice, as an exemplar of the difficulties inherent in the family milieu and the problematic relations between the sexes, and as a gripping narrative that draws the reader into a web of soap-operatic intrigue, the case of Dora has fascinated commentators from an array of perspectives. Since the majority of these writers, as we might expect, fall within the domain of orthodox analysis, our discussion will naturally focus on this. We will also devote some attention to several discussions of the text as literature: To what genre can we assign the psychoanalytic case history, and, more particularly, *this* case history? What problems and contradictions are entailed in this analysis? Dora's situation has also been examined as a political problem, of either economics or sexuality, and we will look at some of the more relevant of these discussions.

We can read the history of *Dora* as a palimpsest (or, to modernize the analogy, a computer disk that has been overwritten). The original interaction (or at least a report of it by one of its participants) still exists, but can no longer be read in isolation, without influence from the immense body of commentary that has accreted over the past century, from many perspectives. There are the orthodox analysts, anxious to discover what went wrong with *this* analysis and reassure themselves and us that the problems do not extend to *all* analyses; the Lacanians, who argue that *Dora* must be seen from Freud's earlier theoretical perspective, rather than his later, ego-oriented framework (the one preferred by the current orthodoxy); text critics, who see in *Dora* the beginnings, however unintended, of new and controversial literary genres; and social critics, Marxists and feminists, who see the contretemps of the consulting room as just a special case of social injustice and inequality: to avoid repetitions of the trauma, society itself must change its views on women, men, families, and power. The case history, moreover, can be (and has been) used both as validation of psychoanalysis and its theoretical constructs and as evidence of the falsity and destructiveness of the intrapsychic model of therapy.

We have already made reference to a spectrum of beliefs within psychotherapy, from strongly intrapsychic to strongly societal, about the cause and appropriate treatment of symptoms. It is useful to situate the writings on *Dora* along that spectrum. We might place Lacanian theory at one end, as the most strongly intrapsychic point on the spectrum. Lacan (e.g., 1966) and his followers argue that Freud went wrong when he abandoned his original model of the psyche, as exemplified most explicitly in *The Interpretation of Dreams* (1900/1953), contrasting conscious, preconscious, and unconscious levels of psychic functioning. Later (e.g., especially in *The Ego and the Id*, 1923/1961) Freud moved away from this to a rather more concrete picture, with the "structural" agencies of id, ego, and superego replacing the former "topographic" version. In his earlier theory, stress on the unconscious as the basis for symptom and symbol formation resulted in a largely intrapsychic understanding of neurosis: Illness came about because the unconscious was unable or unwilling to communicate directly with the conscious, within an individual. Masson (1983) argues that this version itself represents a turning away from an originally more interpersonal model, in which neurosis results from mistreatment of the child by caretakers. Lacan, however, argues for a return to the Freud of the *Interpretation of Dreams*, in which intrapsychic, rather than interpersonal, disturbed relations are the grist for the analytic mill. He and his followers, beginning in the 1940s, see the American and British orthodoxy (including the later Freud) as traitors to the revolution. The original stress on disturbed intrapsychic communication, they argue, was the truly new insight, a subversion of Victorian self-perception and hence threatening to the establishment. Therefore (as, Masson argues, happened with "seduction theory" early on), it was watered down by the introduction of the more practical interpolations of ego psychology and, later, object relations theory. For Lacan, as for Freud, the Oedipus complex was "bedrock," the possession or lack of a phallus (real, symbolic, and imaginary) the major criterion of self-identity. For Lacanian theorists, *Dora* represents a case of broken communication within the patient herself. The patient's anamnesis, dreams, and symptoms are seen as a cryptic "text": To unravel this text, render it explicitly intelligible, is to provide coherency for the patient, which should amount to a "cure." Patient and analyst, Dora and Freud, exist as symbolic representations in each other's minds: Transference and countertransference images (rather than the actual persons themselves) confront each other. The analysis then is an intrapsychic process engaged in individually by both parties parallel to each other and therefore not intersecting.

Though the Lacanians fault current orthodox analytic theory for its retreat from the psyche, yet by other standards it remains quite strongly intrapsychic in its focus: If interpersonal difficulties in communication do exist, they are generally presumed to arise because the patient's id is interfering with normal communicative routes, so the need is to get id and ego back into some sort of good relationship. The ego mediates between reality and id, and so is affected by outside events and tries to protect the id from them or interpret them to the id. So this version of analytic theory recognizes the existence and the influence on the psyche of real others in a real world, but distress is still seen as located within that individual psyche, rather than arising out of the impingements of reality on the patient.

Continuing along our spectrum, and still remaining within the psychoanalytic fold (at least by some standards) are the proponents of cultural psychoanalysis, who see psychic distress as originating in social anomalies, power inequities based on sex and class. Karen Horney, Clara Thompson, and William Alanson White are most frequently mentioned as spearheading this movement. Although they see psychological distress as externally originated, they nonetheless attack it by intrapsychic means, so that they can be considered at least loosely analytically oriented. Since no commentary on *Dora* exists from within this school, we will have no more to say about it here.

The spectrum continues, with psychological models moving further and further from the Lacanian/Freudian unconscious and intrapersonal sphere. As early as the late 1940s, Gregory Bateson and his collaborators began to see psychological distress not only as caused by poor communicative patterns encountered by an individual early in life, but as perpetuated between people in close relationships, contributing to difficulties in those relationships, which in turn created more individual psychic distress. It had been noted by therapists that, if only one member of a couple was satisfactorily treated, while individual distress might lessen, the relationship might also disintegrate—perhaps too high a price to pay for relief of intrapsychic symptoms. So these therapists, going by various names (e.g., family therapists, couple therapists, brief therapists), began to see the unit requiring treatment not as the individual, but as the intimate group: couple or family. The emphasis then shifted from disentangling the root causes of communicative problems via interpretation of the unconscious, to interrupting bad patterns in the here-and-now and implementing alternative modes of communication. The therapist comes to function less as the omniscient exegetical scholar, poring over mysterious texts in foreign languages or secret codes, and more as a coworker with special skills, a teacher with communicative techniques, or an instigator of experiences of new ways of relating—the approach of interpersonal systems theory. While interpersonal therapies are not particularly egalitarian, their authoritarianism is explicit, as opposed to the covert authoritarianism of psychoanalysis.

But what all these schools share is that they are therapies, and as such they believe that people experiencing distress in relationships are the ones on whom treatment should focus, the ones who must change. At the other end of the spectrum are theorists who see the work done in therapy as futile at best, destructive at worst, allowing the true causes of pain to persist unabated; in the worst case, knowingly scapegoating the victims of an unjust and hierarchical system as the "identified patients," the "sick" ones, thereby allowing the powerful to continue with business as usual. Marxist and some feminist criticism of *Dora* takes this position, as do writers on "madness," as an attempt to make sense of a crazy world, such as Laing (1967).

Finally, the discussion encompasses a group that does not fit on the spectrum, since it is unconcerned with therapy as a way of dealing with personal difficulty. Rather, it views psychoanalysis generally, and *Dora* in particular, as exegetical texts. *Dora* is approached by late-twentieth-century psychoanalytic literary critics as their medieval progenitors viewed the Bible, only more onion-like, more layered. Analysis itself is an act of interpretation; Freud is engaged in interpreting Dora's psyche. Now the critic comes upon *Dora* as an anomalous sort of purportedly "scientific" text, one requiring hermeneutic expansion; a hybrid between scientific and humanistic discourse. Some critics stop with that; others, who are also social critics, see *Dora's* cryptic nature as a sign of social malaise: Both the underlying meaning that is revealed to the critic's "picklocks," and the need Freud himself had for unclear exposition, are significant. But all of these, like many therapeutic writers, see the job of therapy, and the work of the commentator on therapeutic texts, as essentially semantic: to find meaning. We argue that therapy and theory must go beyond that level to pragmatics, as must any full understanding of *Dora*. So while we start from a text, acknowledging the need to do semantic exegesis on several levels in order to understand what happened, we depart from strict textual interpretation in also focusing on *Dora* as a description of an interpersonal event, and on Dora's distress as both interpersonally and societally based, its failure intelligible as deriving from a violation of normal communicative principles.

Let us return to a brief examination of previous work on *Dora*, to see more explicitly the range of discussion and the place of the present text. Within the analytic tradition, numerous commentators since Freud have essentially taken his position, altering it slightly but keeping to the idea that the failure of the case lay in one or another aspect of the transference (or the countertransference, essentially the same perspective). It is interesting that virtually all the discussion of the case has occurred since the 1960s, possibly because (as Jennings, 1986, suggests) it was around that time that the issues of transference and countertransference—the conduct of the therapeutic relationship itself, as opposed to the analyst's mental work of interpretation—began to receive strong emphasis in analytic writing. More to the point, by the late 1960s feminist critics of psychoanalysis not only (like the others) were using *Dora* to illustrate to readers within the field the dangers of psychoanalysis, but were disseminating their views in writing meant for the general public—including prospective patients.

Jennings (1986) provides a useful overview and summary of all the writing on *Dora* through 1985. As a psychoanalyst, he tends to focus his examination on that area, omitting discussion of much of the feminist criticism. One valuable aspect of this article is its summary chart of recurrent themes in the corpus (e.g., transference/countertransference, Dora as female patient, *Dora* as literary text).

Certain individual writings have been especially influential. Within psychoanalysis itself, Muslin and Gill (1978) comment both on aspects of the transference that Freud left unanalyzed and on the countertransference (which Freud did not explicitly recognize at all) as complicating the case. The authors suggest that the negative transference (which Freud did not discuss, at least under the name of transference) was at least as much a problem as the unresolved positive or erotic transference that is the focus of Freud's interpretation. Further, the authors note that much of Freud's behavior in the case, particularly considering the mores of the period, could be taken as countertransference—or in fact more than countertransference, realistically viewed as attempts at sexual seduction: "But over and above this issue [transference interpretations], there is evidence of Freud's personal blindness to the implicit libidinal interplay between himself and Dora" (Muslin & Gill, 1978, p. 323). There are two problems to consider: The motivation behind Freud's seductiveness, and the extent to which he was unaware of it and its role in undermining the therapy. Another point made by these authors is that Freud, while eventually at least confronting the paternal transference, never recognizes the role of the maternal transference in the case.

Elsewhere in the literature, other aspects of the transference/countertransference are explored. Lewin's (1974) discussion is typical of the approach: He asks what interpretations were not made, what aspects of Dora's transference not covered by Freud. He suggests that Dora's relationship with women, and with her mother in particular, could have been more fully examined. He argues that Dora, as a child, was rebuffed in favor of her brother in her search for her mother's love. Disappointed in this, she ended up envying men, and therefore frustrating and destroying them (p. 520f). From this already somewhat tendentious suggestion it is but a small jump for Lewin to his conclusion: Dora's primary sexual identity was homosexual. "In the light of current knowledge, however, Dora's lack of sexual pleasure at Herr K's kiss might be an accurate weathervane of the direction of Dora's sexual aims. Her sexual objects were women and only women. Men did not turn Dora on, then or ever" (p. 521f). There are many things to criticize in this approach, one being that it implicitly supports Freud's position that only pathology would lead a woman to treat a man such as Herr K (or Freud) so badly. Another is that it overlooks important contradictory evidence such as that in Dora's second dream—an expensive way for an analyst to assuage Freud's ruffled masculinity. A pragmatist might note the abrupt shift in linguistic level, from academese to the slang of "turn on," and could reasonably interpret the shift as a sign of its author's overly personal involvement. Finally, Lewin examines Dora's relationship with her mother.

> Dora's conflicts are the conflicts of all girls growing up, craving their mothers, envying their fathers' primacy, wishing all rivals out of the way, while at the same time trying to retain their roles within their families as loving daughters and sisters. In order to convert their homosexual love for their mothers into heterosexual love for their fathers and for eventual mates, they must develop the defense mechanism of displacement that goes with sublimation. (p. 531f)

This is all quite uncontroversial from a psychoanalytic standpoint, but someone less analytically inclined might note that the author sees Dora's problem from an exclusively masculine point of view, and the difficulties with her analysis as due to incomplete interpretation of the transference (here, maternal).

A more recent book, McCaffrey (1984), focuses on *Dora* from a traditional psychoanalytic perspective, but uses the text as a basis for the comparison of theories of dream interpretation, therefore remaining largely in the semantic realm: It is concerned with the "meaning" of Dora's symptoms and dream-symbols. But Chapter 5, "The Ideology of Sex," is concerned with pragmatic issues—Dora's social and psychological context as a woman. Dora could not accept any of the options offered to her as a young woman, a member of her society, her milieu and her family. " . . . Having rejected the demeaning roles offered her by the adults, she could imagine no other options. She might reject the past indignantly, but she was unable to construct a future" (McCaffrey, 1984, p. 117).

Marcus (1975), commenting on the case from a literary and sociocultural (and heavily psychoanalytic) perspective, concentrates mostly on Freud's interpretations themselves. While noting with approval Freud's perspicacity, he does not—any more than did Freud himself—notice what Freud left out of his interpretations: For instance, any recognition that there are issues referable not to intrapsychic confusion on Dora's part, but to the covert difficulties inherent in her milieu, for example, the contempt in which women are held, particularly Dora's mother, by members of her circle; and Herr K's rather interesting probable sexual preferences, to be discussed later.

Toward the end of his discussion, Marcus approaches the question of what went wrong. He alludes to the problem of the unanalyzed transference, and then remarks on the countertransference.

> He doesn't like her negative sexuality, her inability to surrender to her own erotic impulses. He doesn't like her "really remarkable achievements in the direction of intolerable behavior." He doesn't like her endless reproachfulness. Above all, he doesn't like her inability to surrender herself to him. For what Freud was as yet unprepared to face was not merely the transference, but the counter-transference as well—in the case of Dora, it was largely a negative counter-transference—an unanalyzed part of himself. (p. 108)

This is still viewing the problems in the case as intrapsychic, confined to the therapeutic situation. To attribute part of the failure of the analysis to unanalyzed countertransference is to suggest that, had Freud known himself better, the disaster could have been averted.

All these discussions examine the case as if Freud and Dora did not have any realistic, direct experience of each other—knew each other only through their ideas, if that. Moreover, they do not take into consideration that Dora was entangled in a bizarre family situation, and that certain duties and expectations, explicit and otherwise, devolving upon her and dividing her loyalties, played havoc with her sense of personal worth and identity and circumscribed her growth. Although Freud alludes to these circumstances from time to time in his narrative, he gives no indication that he ever communicated to Dora his compassion, much less his understanding of the bind she is caught in. Indeed, his interpretations tend to suggest that she has willingly, if unconsciously, created the situation for herself and that she is reveling in it. Occasional writers have commented on the anguish of Dora's reality and its relation to her symptoms—without, however, examining Freud's role in exacerbating her distress by implicitly legitimizing the behavior of the adults in her surroundings.

One such analytic commentator, Blos (1972), suggests that the difficulty arises unavoidably in the very business of making interpretations to adolescents: "If there is one thing analysis has taught us, it is that ill-timed interpretations are unconsciously experienced by the adolescent as a parental—that is, incestuous—seduction" (p. 130).

Since Dora had been subjected to incestuous seductions so often and so traumatically in the past, Freud's interpretive behavior could only be seen by her as a repetition of the same theme, and a reinforcement of what she already had good enough reason to believe about men. Certainly we would concur with Blos that Freud's interpretations to Dora were ill-timed: The analysis itself went on for only 3 months, and he proceeded to make his very deep, indeed invasive, interpretations almost at once.

In a deservedly famous paper, another analytic commentator, Erikson (1962), argues sensitively that Dora's illness was, in some sense, an adaptive strategy—her only way of dealing with the betrayals and seductions that constituted her environment. Erikson suggests further that Freud's insistence that Dora's concern for the historical truth was merely a resistance to uncovering the (far more important) "genetic truth" of her illness may have done her damage, coming as it did during her adolescence, when she was desperately feeling a need to determine for herself what was real, who was to be trusted, and who taken as a model.

> The question arises whether today we would consider a patient's emphasis on the historical truth a mere matter of resistance to the genetic one; or whether we would discern in it also an adaptive pattern genuine for her stage of life, and challenged by her circumstances. (Erikson, 1962, p. 465f)

In other words, Dora did the best she could to arrive at maturity in circumstances that discouraged health; and Freud did her a disservice by not acknowledging that her symptoms were an outgrowth of her striving toward health and maturity, not merely a regressive expression of the failure to resolve her Oedipus complex. Erikson notes, too, that some of the purely intrapsychic interpretations Freud makes, for example, of Dora's dreams, could be insightfully extended by considering them expressions of her personal, and interpersonal, dilemma, not atypical of adolescence. In her first dream, the "house" and "jewel case," in addition to the sexual significance Freud attributes to them, also "represent the adolescent quandary: if there is a 'fire' in 'our house' (that is, in our family), then what 'valuables' (that is, values) shall be saved first?" (Erikson, 1962, p. 461). If we see Dora's symptoms, including her "truly intolerable behavior" toward Freud and everyone else, as attempts to preserve her own integrity and discover what, in her family's values, she can believe in, we get a rather different picture of her case from that which Freud wished the reader to see.

Rieff (1963) discusses some of Dora's interpersonal as well as intrapsychic problems in his introduction to the case history.

> The sick daughter has a sick father, who has a sick mistress, who has a sick husband, who proposes himself to the sick daughter as her lover. Dora does not want to hold hands in this charmless circle—although Freud, does, at one point, indicate that she should. . . . My point here is that all the others are also cases, so to speak, the very predicates of Dora's; and yet, they are, except in minor ways, inaccessible to Freud. Moreover, Freud accepts this inaccessibility without serious theoretical question. His entire interpretation of the case—and also his efforts to reindoctrinate Dora in more tolerable attitudes toward her own sex life—depends upon his limiting the case to Dora when, in fact, from the evidence he himself presents, it is the milieu in which she is constrained to live that is ill. Here is a limit on the psychoanalytic therapy that neither Freud nor his orthodox followers have examined with the ruthless honesty appropriate to their ethic. "Milieu" therapy would involve a revolution in our culture. (p. 10)

This is getting closer to the point on what has gone wrong, since it concentrates on Freud's failure to touch or change those in Dora's environment, rather than on his treatment of Dora herself.

*Dora* has been viewed, over the years, from perspectives other than the psychoanalytic. For some commentators, it has served as the example *par excellence* of the case history—whether this is seen as a literary form (Marcus, 1975) or as a scientific "exemplar" in the Kuhnian sense (Pletsch, 1982), a guide for beginning practitioners. For everyone who has commented on it, *Dora* seems to be a special kind of example, a clarifying and defining case for whatever thesis the writer is attempting to prove. And certainly *Dora* has the hypnotic effect of a first-rate novel on any reader.

Marcus sees the psychoanalytic case history as a new form of literary narrative, not coincidentally developed in a period of literary experimentation with the role and reliability of the narrator, and the narrator's relation to other characters as well as the reader. He sees *Dora* as bearing certain resemblances to the modern experimental novel, in point of its "plastic, involuted and heterogeneous" (pp. 263–264) structure, its "inner logic that frequently seems to be at odds with itself" (p. 264). "Its continuous innovations in formal structure," Marcus writes, seem unavoidably to be dictated by its substance, by the dangerous, audacious, disreputable, and problematical character of the experiences being represented and dealt with, and the equally scandalous intentions of the author and the outrageous character of the role he has had the presumption to assume. (p. 264)

This is fascinating stuff, to the literary mind; but if Marcus's arguments are correct, how can we interpret *Dora* as a scientific document written as an example of how psychotherapy works, by a man who is trying to establish his field as scientifically responsible, its results predictable (as Pletsch would have it)? If it is true that we are drawn into the case history as into a Gothic novel, with what point of view are we to emerge from it? A document is to be read either as a piece of fact (or science) or a piece of fiction, not both. The one informs, the other entertains. The conventions of the two genres, as well as the needs and expectations of the readers of each, are necessarily quite different.

Writings in the recently created genre sometimes called "faction,"[1] encompassing, for instance, Norman Mailer's *Armies of the Night* and Truman Capote's *In Cold Blood*, are only in part counterexamples to this argument. Both of these were written to entertain rather than to educate and inform, so that it is in a sense only an extra thrill for the reader to realize that there is a factual basis to the exciting narrative. A work, however grounded in fact, written with the aim of entertaining is less likely to pose a problem to scientific truth than is a work intended pedagogically, but employing some of the conventions of fiction—Marcus's view of *Dora*. Reading fiction (Nabokov's *Lolita*, for instance), we are delighted when the purported author/narrator represents himself as scurrilous and unreliable, and we, the readers, must sort through the text like detectives to decide as best we can where truth lies. But if a scientist—physical or social—attempts the same trick, how can we take him seriously as a scientist? And *Dora* is a veritable bag of narrative tricks. We might go so far as to suggest that the very brilliancy of the text as literary matter raises a troubling moral issue: Dare the therapist make light of actual suffering by making it ambiguous, and therefore interesting, to the reader? And more: While it is accepted therapeutic practice to "fictionalize" case histories to some extent to protect identities, how far can "fictionalization" go without making a mockery of the history-as-exemplar, as teaching tool? Can the therapist learn how to deal with depression by reading *Hamlet*? Perhaps, but only if it is clear that Hamlet himself is a literary confection, not someone who could have existed in life. There is a contradiction between Marcus's view of the case history as experimental fiction, and that of Pletsch, case history as a scientific example of truthful narrative.

Pletsch suggests that case histories function for psychotherapy as exemplary cases do for the natural sciences. A case history, by giving students in a field a glimpse of how assumptions in that field are organized and experienced in real working life, breathes life into cold textbook principles. As he says,

> As important vehicles of the tradition of psychoanalytic knowledge, Freud's case studies still communicate essential knowledge to psychoanalysts today. . . . What psychoanalysts derive from their study of Freud's cases is a sense of how Freud thought, more particularly, how he thought with his patients. Even to the nonpsychoanalytic reader, Freud's case studies seem to communicate how it feels to do psychoanalysis and to learn from patients. (p. 102)

Then for Pletsch, the case history is truth, information about the reality of psychoanalysis, training in doing the day-to-day work. Case histories are what give psychoanalysis its link to the scientific method and bolster its claims to scientific objectivity. Perhaps the metapsychological theory cannot be substantiated, psychoanalysts might argue: But the case histories at least prove that the method—at least some of the time—works! They are the records of Kuhnian normal science.

For psychoanalysts, who delight in considering their field an "art-science," such discussion can only be titillating. But the problems of a field that straddles these aspects of human consciousness are as often ignored as the pleasures are celebrated. If the case history is, in at least some salient respects, untruthful, how can it possibly function as the bearer of official scientific validity? If it is necessarily false in its presentation, how can it be falsified?

Psychoanalysis itself obscures the distinction represented by Marcus and Pletsch, having been defined by its founder as an "art-science," an uneasy dichotomy that followers have clutched fondly to their breasts as embodying the best of both worlds. But psychoanalysts, including Freud, would, if forced to make a choice, surely assign themselves to the "science" camp, for reasons we discuss in Chapter 6.

Several commentators from within and outside psychoanalysis look at *Dora* as exemplifying some of the difficulties created by the "art-science" categorization. Interpretation, that cynosure of the field—the reason psychoanalysis enjoys the continuing interest and respect of academics in the humanities and social sciences—is the crux of the problem. Interpretation is, to be sure, the pivot on which the "art-science" assignment turns. Interpretation is as well the basis of literary criticism; and also that of much work in anthropology, sociology, and psychology, whether or not the fact is explicitly recognized. Modern linguistics would not exist without it, as it underlies the so-called Chomskyan revolution. (We shall say more on this in later chapters.) In the humanities, interpretation has been seen as a mentalistic enterprise, not subject to the constraints of science. But within the social sciences, and most strongly of all in psychoanalysis with its adherence to the medical model, interpretation has been seen as a version of scientific method, as analogous to medical interventions that are scientifically testable. In Popper's (1962) term, psychoanalysis sees interpretation as falsifiable.

Edelson (1975) and Spence (1982, 1986) discuss the use of *interpretation* in psychoanalysis as contrasted with *explanation* in the natural sciences. They note that in its desire to be "scientific," psychoanalysis tends to conflate the two, but that in fact there are crucial differences between them. Explanation, Edelson argues, generalizes; interpretation is specific to the case at hand. As a result, scientific explanations are predictive (one case is relevant to others in the future), thus testable, therefore falsifiable. This is not so of interpretation. Spence notes that explanation relies on publicly available information and rules of evidence, as well as using logic shared by most members of a culture; interpretation is based on privately held beliefs and idiosyncratic inferential processes. Psychoanalysis, they argue, should at least be clear about how its methods work and what they imply.

If these questions seem liable to get us into a dangerously speculative and mentalistic view of *Dora*, a good corrective is to be found in those works that approach it from a political perspective, focusing on how Dora's position in the real world affects her power in the analytic situation and finally governs its outcome. *Dora* can thus be read as social commentary. Not only was the family situation described in the case history unique to, and symptomatic of, a particular time and place, but the interpretations and responses of the author-narrator are similarly bound by cultural context. Freud, while in so many ways a daring pioneer, and so often willing to risk scorn and rejection for espousing unpopular ideas, in other ways was very much a man of his times, unable to see much beyond their social strictures and hypocrisies, and willing, all too often, to use his influence to protect that shaky system. His blindness in the area of female psychology and relations between the sexes has been commented on by feminist authors.

Two of the strongest cases are made by Mary Daly (1978) in *Gyn/Ecology* and Phyllis Chesler (1972) in *Women and Madness*. Both make essentially the same points: that Freud, as a male caught in Victorian patriarchal assumptions, misdiagnosed the patient and perceived as her illness what rightly was the illness, or viciousness, of her family circle; that, by allowing himself to remain blinded to Dora's very real predicament and by legitimizing the treachery being carried on all about her by those she loved, Freud not only ensured Dora's continued illness and essentially destroyed her as a woman and a human being, but also brought aid and comfort to a social system that oppressed women and children for the aggrandizement of men. The narrator of *Dora* can be seen as a predator in helper's clothing, as a man who takes a woman's trust and uses it for her destruction—for the sake of supporting a social structure that benefits men alone, at women's expense.

There has been other discussion of the case from a feminist perspective. A recent collection (Bernheimer & Kahane, 1985) brings together many of the papers written over the past century on *Dora*, both the old classics and more recent, especially feminist, rethinkings. Among the latter are papers by Collins, Green, Lydon, Sachner, and Skoller (1983), Gallop (1982), Gearhart (1979), Hertz (1983), Moi (1981), Ramas (1980), Rose (1978), and Sprengnether (1985).

The papers in this collection form an important and fascinating set. In her introduction, Claire Kahane notes that the rise of feminism and the development of new theories of text come together to permit new readings of *Dora*.

For the feminist project that took shape in the late 1960s was to reexamine the cultural assumptions about femininity and female desire and to describe how those assumptions contributed to the circumscription of women. The Dora case is a particularly rich gift to this project: a paradigmatic text of patriarchal assumptions about

female desire that still carry cultural authority and a vivid record
of the construction of those assumptions as they emerge from the
desire of the interpreter. Even more provocatively, the traces of
Dora's story that form a subtext to Freud's oedipal narrative and
continually disrupt it suggest an alternative preoedipal narrative
that many feminists are reinscribing. (pp. 24–25)

While new ways of interpreting *Dora* offer rich new understandings, we would argue that a truly feminist critique must re-
frame the text itself, go beyond or above or beneath it. Freud's
and Dora's needs from each other go beyond the relations of the
consulting room. They echo the unresolved problems inherent in
male–female relations everywhere. Some of the papers approach
the question, but from the purely semantic perspective characteristic of literary criticism. These do to Freud (and *Dora*) what
Freud did to Dora: superimpose their own pre-existing text, force
particular readings. They veer between matter that *is* actually patent in the text and what can, or could, or might possibly, be read
in; between interpretations that are beyond question and those
that are, to be polite, highly idiosyncratic (like so many of Freud's)
and unjustified by anything in the text itself (like so many of
Freud's). Carried away by semantic, intertextual ingenuity, it
is all too easy to create dazzling meta-text, in which *Dora* is the
basis of the (tertiary) author's fantasy, even as Freud in his "scientific" secondary text creation produced text more characteristic
of poesy than science.

A problem is posed by Kahane's definition of *Dora* in the
passage above as primarily concerned with "patriarchal assumptions about female desire," as reflected in "the desire of the interpreter." Sexuality, so characteristic of Lacanian thought, while
certainly relevant to a part of Dora's dilemma, is, if made the
centerpiece of the argument, more than a little reductionist. Yes,
*Dora* is about the misattribution and misinterpretation of its pro-
tagonist's emergent sexuality. But it is even more poignantly
about the thwarting of her intellectual curiosity, her capacity for
trust, and her ability to form lasting friendships. By forcing her
into a sexual cubbyhole, Freud, Lacan, and their followers deny a
significant aspect of Dora's being. We hardly need note that
women, over the millennia, have been much more victimized by
this sort of reductionist stereotyping than men.

One can cite as exemplary Gallop's delightful and imaginative
discussion of *Dora* as "Door-a," providing Freud with the "key"

that is one of the "picklocks" of the case. The temptation for the English-speaking writer is great; but what exactly does the interpolation of "Door-a" tell us about the actual analytic situation? For the German-speaking protagonists, it is a dangerous leap to suppose that any such connection was implicit, much less natural; there is no clue in the primary text itself. So Gallop is creating a fantasy on *Dora*, on what it suggests to her, the tertiary creator of text. But it is less clear that this reading can be presented as illuminating Freud's, or Dora's own, experience, or indeed the analytic experience.

Or consider the discussion in several papers (especially Marcus, 1975, and Hertz, 1983) that link Freud's style and content to Dora's, in the latter case explicitly suggesting an identification between the two. They speak, for instance, of the hysteric's typically incomplete or incoherent narrative, and relate that to Freud's "fragment," replete as it is with questionable conclusions and other unreliabilities. Is Freud taking on Dora's hysterical persona? Are the two identities being merged, narrator and subject fusing? An intriguing reading, to be sure—but again, not so useful in our understanding of the events the text purports to portray. For surely the kinds of incompletenesses and anomalies Dora as storyteller displays are different in every way from Freud's; and their reasons for incompleteness differ as well. We are dealing, we might say, with a relation of homonymy, accidental formal similarity, rather than any true equivalence. Just as a pun (which is based on accidental homonymy) is ingenious but seldom revealing of any great depth, so such interpretations coruscate, but fail to illumine. The pragmatics of the situation are cast aside for the sake of semantic identity, which in turn leads to questionable semantics.

These papers in the volume, then, re-examine the case history from three major perspectives: (1) scrutinizing the text for signs of Freud's unconscious identification with Dora—a sort of "identification with the aggressee" (Hertz and Marcus); (2) searching for signs of Freud's patriarchal biases, a move away from the pure text itself (Sprengnether, Moi, and Ramas); and finally (3) turning the tables with an analysis of Freud himself, reading *Dora* taking Freud, rather than Dora, as the producer of the primary text. Freud can be seen as one much in need of analysis (hopefully, not by him): a man out of touch with, and in great fear of, femininity, his own and that of others in his environment (Collins et al. and Moi).

For those of us who find the insights elsewhere in Freud's work invaluable, it is tempting—as some feminist apologists for Freud have tried to do (e.g., Mitchell, 1974, and, more persuasively, Decker, 1990)—to overlook his views on women exemplified in *Dora*; to argue that Freud's assumptions, however mistaken, arose out of the world in which he grew up and lived, and that, as long as we are beyond that now, we can forgive and forget, eliminating from psychoanalytic theory and practice its oppressive aspects (which can be shorn off as mere excrescences) and salvaging the truths that are inherent. Other feminist critics, and we in the balance of our discussion, would argue otherwise: The short-sightedness of those parts of psychoanalytic theory that concern female psychology not only so permeates the whole that it is impossible to expunge, but informs and indeed creates the therapeutic method and many of the interpretive assumptions that are the backbone of all individual, insight-oriented therapies: One has no existence without the other. There is a reasonable middle ground: Freud, as a man of his time, can be excused for lack of vision. But the incorporation of ancient misogyny into a field that claims to develop via the scientific method, and the inability of that field to rid itself of short-sighted doctrines of this kind, suggest a serious flaw in theory and method.

Like feminists, Marxists have been critics of psychoanalysis, on somewhat similar grounds. Both groups argue that Freud assigns to patients the sickness that belongs to their social milieu, whether on a sexual or an economic basis. To analyze an individual, to interpret individual distress as based on a private and personal trauma, is to exculpate the real offenders and guarantee the preservation of the status quo—and thus to bring no real relief to the suffering. Taking this position, Lichtman (1982) sees Dora's predicament as arising out of a paternalistic family milieu, but also suggests that blaming the family is little better than assigning the problem to the individual. The family is corrupt because of its role in a corrupt capitalistic society. Capitalism necessarily oppresses women and children, allowing economically successful men to get away with, and get approval for, their psychic tyranny over their families as well as their economic oppression of less powerful members of society at large. For Lichtman, then—as for many feminist critics, though on different grounds—the solution to Dora's problems lies in radical social reorganization, not individual psychotherapy.

Most of the commentators we have cited see the therapist's

role as treating Dora, as the identified patient, "bringing her to reason." But a few writers identify the problem as outside the patient, in her milieu, and argue that altering that, in one way or another, is the only appropriate therapeutic intervention.

Writing in 1974, Maddi, as a family therapist, is one of the earliest to see *Dora* as a documentation of victimization of the powerless by her more powerful milieu. "I regard Freud's approach as both unethical and unesthetic," he says.

> . . . . As I read Freud's account of Dora, I find a beleaguered, overwhelmed youngster caught in a fantastic web of corruption constructed by all the important adults in her life. . . . [Freud] makes it clear that he believes her account. . . . But he accepts [the adults'] attribution of the sexual problem to Dora herself, and sets about convincing her of her guilt with all the manipulative weaponry of psychoanalysis. (p. 99)

Maddi further suggests that Freud "could have precipitated a confrontation among [the adults in Dora's milieu] in his presence, or even counseled her to leave her corrupt home for college" (p. 100). But as Decker (1990) makes clear, breaking off relations with her family was out of the question, practically as well as emotionally, for a young woman in Dora's position, in Dora's society. Nor would provoking a confrontation have been an acceptable, or even comprehensible, form of therapy for a middle-class Viennese family of 1900, when rigid formality and distance were the rule in professional relationships. Even today, confrontational tactics are widely viewed as dangerous, to be used with extreme caution and only by therapists with great skill—and ours is a society that sets a high value on directness and spontaneity.

Stierlin (1976) makes the point that Freud's intrapsychic emphasis, while necessary to his own theoretical development, led to distortion and error, as in Dora's case.

Finally, Decker (1990) looks at *Dora* from the perspective of the larger society in which she, and her family, were situated. As a young Jewish woman in a society both anti-Semitic and misogynistic, Dora may have found the double bias too much to contend against. With only one such strike against him, Dora's brother could break out of the stifling family situation and establish himself in the world; as Heilbrun (1990, pp. 38ff) suggests, Karen Horney might have found it easier to escape from Freudian misogyny than did her female analytic colleagues such as Helene Deutsch, because almost alone she was Christian.

In the chapters that follow, we attempt to fit all these disparate perspectives into a whole, partly by superimposing on Dora's story two more frameworks: that of linguistic pragmatics, and that of interpersonal systems theory. Both are concerned with the patterns individuals and groups use to convey ideas to others, their choices of appropriate and inappropriate, effective and ineffective strategies; and the ways in which their choices are often circumscribed by their gender and position in society, as well as their position within the family milieu.

Pragmatic theorists, like interpersonal theorists and therapists, are interested in therapeutic dialogue as a discourse type: how it is learned, how it is manipulated by the participants, how it is similar to and different from other types of conversations, and why it is efficacious in creating change. So from these perspectives we can do what other commentators have not—focus on the communicative aspect of the analytic experience. What was it like for Dora, and for Freud, to participate in the dialogue recorded in Freud's history? Why did Freud choose this way of talking to Dora? How did Dora respond? How do we sift the half-spoken undertones; and how do we deal with the levels of direct and indirect communication—that recognized within Dora's family circle, as well as that developed between the participants in the analysis itself? Did the analysis function—as it should—as a corrective communicative model, or as yet another example for Dora of adult communicative untrustworthiness?

There has been much written within the psychoanalytic framework on communication between analyst and patient. But as with discussion of interpretation, it has been semantic in focus: how is a patient's oblique comment to be translated back to him or her? How is the Basic Rule to be utilized? We are suggesting a pragmatic perspective. We assume that the way in which each of the participants communicates arises out of, and alters, the real-world relationship in which they exist. To speak of transference and countertransference puts the analytic discourse on a purely, and deceptively, semantic basis; we must also see what is happening as an actual conversation with real implications for the participants.

On the basis of this discussion, we argue that the problems in Freud's treatment of Dora were deeper than his previous critics have seen, a failure not remediable by improvements in analytic technique, though those might be steps in the right direction. The damage did not come from the interpretations themselves, nor their timing, and indeed there is no clear reason to dispute any of Freud's interpretations of the material: Everything he said might have been right, although there is little corroboration of any of his interpretations.[2] But the rightness or wrongness of the interpretations is irrelevant for us. What matters is the communicative use to which they were put: how Freud intended them to affect Dora, what he was communicating to her about his relationship to her, and about her role in the therapy and in her future life, by his manner of interpreting and communicating to her. We cannot say that Freud intended consciously that his interpretations have the effect they did; but they did have an effect, and it is important for us, as possible past, present, or future participants in the business of psychotherapy, or in the society it affects, to understand how that effect is brought about, for good or bad. We suggest that the problems we find in the conduct of this case are a natural and frequently irresistible hazard for the therapist engaged in intrapsychically oriented individual therapy; and that these hazards are so serious and so easy to fall into that the outcome of *Dora* casts doubt on the validity and safety of psychoanalytic technique in general.

## NOTES

1. In writings in this genre, the author takes a real-life event—often, as in these examples, an especially lurid crime—as the basis of the writing. But rather than restrict descriptions to facts available in the public record, or even interviews, the author makes assumptions and interpretations of protagonists' thoughts, motives, and actions. In that sense the genre is "fiction," since the writer is inventing, rather than reporting, at least some aspects of reality.

2. The problem of the corroboration of psychoanalytic interpretations has been addressed both by analysts (e.g., Strachey, 1934) and philosophers of science (e.g., Grünbaum, 1984). Strachey suggests specific kinds of data that can be thought of as verifying interpretations, while Grünbaum argues that (given the peculiarities of the analytic relationship) analytic interpretations cannot be confirmed by the sort of evidence that Strachey suggests, nor indeed in any other known way.

In fact, the case is even worse. The existence of the psychoanalytic tenet of "overdetermination," combined with the various "out's" utilized by analysts to explain why apparently correct interpretations don't produce improvement (e.g., flight into illness, viscosity of the libido, negative therapeutic reaction, resistance, negative transference), plus the doctrine that the patient is always wrong when not in agreement with the analyst (a doctrine modern analysts claim to reject, but often make covert use of), guarantee that *no* interpretation can ever be proven true—much less falsified. So one end of the scientific method, hypothesis-formation, is invalidated by overdetermination, precluding a scientific statement; the other, falsification, is rendered impossible by the various excuses for the weak linkage between interpretation and change. (We will discuss in Chapter 5 this and other problems of interpretation in psychoanalysis.)

# 4

# Some Linguistic Background

People have a self-contradictory view of language. On the one hand, proverbs and legends encode our belief that it is powerful, it changes things. In scores of myths and fairy tales, speaking the "magic words" brings success; the wrong words, disaster. At the same time, we distinguish between words and actions: Actions speak louder than words, words are mere fluff. It is a problematic dichotomy for all kinds of language use, but the more so for therapy, which occupies a curious position within the self-contradiction: Therapy is action done almost totally by words, words that themselves create change. What distinguishes one therapeutic theory or method from another is, above all else, how each deals with language: how client and therapist are to communicate, what they may say to each other, what language means and how it creates change. Other institutions, of course, use language to get their work done. But only psychotherapy makes language itself both the object and means of its workings.

The relationship between therapy and language goes deeper still. Starting with Freud, most theorists in the field of talking therapy see language, or communication, as the basis of the client or patient's distress, miscommunication as the source of symptoms, or indeed the symptom itself. Once the field of psychiatry saw language as having an even wider influence in the causation of psychic distress than most practitioners would today. In the 1960s and 1970s, for instance, probably the majority would have held that poor communication between parent and child underlay schizophrenia and its sufferers' bizarre communicative patterns.[1] While today this assumption is much less fashionable, in psychic problems of lesser magnitude it is still taken for granted, and reasonably so, that poor communication strategies—of one sort or another, by parents or significant others—are the root of psychic difficulty.

Then it is curious that so little attention is paid within the therapeutic community to developments in linguistic theory. This absence is particularly striking in psychoanalysis proper—striking because language plays an even more dominant role there than in other therapeutic models. While Freud himself, as a clinician, often displays a remarkably subtle analytic ear for language as his patients use it, as a theorist his writings (e.g., 1910/1957) on language per se demonstrate a naivete unusual even for his times. The absence of linguistic sophistication is continued in the works of most of his followers, even as they talk about their patients' idiosyncratic ways of speaking, though perhaps it makes more sense to relate this aberration not to a willful avoidance of the findings of this one obscure field, but rather to the tendency of psychoanalysis to avoid contamination from almost all other fields of knowledge. But rather than complaining about the effects of linguistic ignorance, it makes more sense to provide a brief background of the linguistic theories and concepts that we will use elsewhere in this discussion, and that may prove useful more generally in understanding the special workings of language in therapeutic settings, as well as the use and misuse of language by all speakers.

The absence of rapprochement between psychoanalysis and linguistics is all the more remarkable because of their close affinities—methodological, theoretical, and (if we can apply this term to a discipline) psychopathological. Both have been obsessed with transmuting the baser metal of humanistic understanding of psychological process into the gold of "scientific" observation; both have set for themselves a similar, and probably similarly impossible, project: the translation into "objective" and "empirical" terms of the subjective and mentalistic operations observable through language use. Both begin with superficially accessible data: language as uttered by a subject in a specific context. For both, that superficial form is of relatively little interest in itself, but only as a "window to the mind," a clue about how the speaker sees the world, internal and external. But the paradox for both is this: the deeper the level of interpretation, the farther one moves from the verifiability of the surface form, the more "subjective" and "unscientific" the results. Moreover, the farther one moves into subjective depths, the more clearly linguistic behavior is seen to be continuous rather than discrete, incapable of sharp taxonomy, and indeterminate—unscientizable, in other words. Yet the deeper the analysis, the more interesting—but unprovable—the results. The closer to the surface, the more responsible and respectable, for the modern social scientist, but also the less the results tell us about the human condition—the reason for the enterprise.

The two fields likewise both wish to represent themselves as "empirical" in method—that is, using externally produced data that is interpreted via quantitative study—yet both are dependent on intuitive or subjective methods. Some mind, the investigator's, subject's or patient's, must interpret the linguistic forms, give them meaning.

Like Freud, Noam Chomsky, the progenitor of modern linguistics, straddles a fuzzy line between determinacy and unpredictability; science and art; empiricism and mentalism. Both heavily influenced related fields in the humanities and social sciences. The passion of both men to be scientists, coupled with the basic unscientizability of much of their subject matter, induces at best confusion and at worst denial or despair in their followers who take them literally. One can see in these requirements and the confusion they necessarily engender the emotional as well as intellectual seeds of postmodernism—although neither would be especially happy with this attribution of paternity.

In both, perhaps because of the failure to impose sufficiently rigorous "scientific" standards, it is possible to observe a sort of nervous machismo: an undervaluation of the work women do or the way women are, within or outside the field itself. And in each the original monolithic field has shattered into a theoretical continuum: in the case of psychoanalysis, from Lacan to Horney, representing the poles of the relation between the mind and the outside world; in the case of transformational generative grammar, from MIT to Berkeley, embodying the poles of the perception of language, from autonomous to heavily interdependent with social and other psychological forces. While the two developments are not genetically related, there are certainly analogies between them.

Linguistic organization spans many levels, from the concrete and small-scale one of sounds (phonology) to the abstract and larger area of discourse analysis. The latter will be most relevant here, allowing entree into the psychological and social concomitants of language use, representing the relationships among language form, intention, and understanding. These considerations reflect the areas of syntax and semantics, but most crucially, pragmatics.

*Syntax* studies sentence form: what words may co-occur, in what order, to form a grammatical sentence of a language. It is what is meant by references to "grammar" and "constructions" in grade school. Speakers of a language implicitly know that certain combinations of words in that language produce meaningful sentences, but others do not (syntacticians mark such ungrammatical sentences with asterisks).

(1a)  Mary admires sincerity.
(1b)  *Sincerity admires Mary.

Speakers make the distinction between the grammatical (1a) and the ungrammatical (1b) with ease, although they have never encountered (1b), and perhaps not (1a) in that form. Or, to take another pair in which the distinction is less dependent on semantics, and more obviously specific to English:

(2a)  John threw it out.
(2b)  *John threw out it.

It should be noted that the technical linguistic definition of "grammaticality" hinges on what *is*, as opposed to what *is not*, actually said by competent speakers. Compare this with the sense of "ungrammatical" we learned in school: Sentences are called "ungrammatical" if they are in fact used, but aren't "good English." The third pair illustrates this distinction, with which linguistics is less concerned.

(3a)  Nobody has seen a unicorn.
(3b)  Aint nobody seen no unicorn.

Often, speakers may have a choice among alternative syntactic patterns to express roughly the same idea. For instance, (4a) and (4b) are paraphrases of each other: One would never be true if the other was false (although one might be appropriate in a context in which the other was not).

(4a)  The boy hit the ball.
(4b)  The ball was hit by the boy.

Syntactic rules are not all we need to know in order to speak a language competently. Meaning and function must be considered. We need to be able to describe the relationship between active sentences (*The boy hit the ball*) and their passive counterparts (*The ball was hit by the boy*), not only as permutations of words, but as choices with communicative consequences. If sentences (4a) and (4b) were fully equivalent, why would speakers ever choose the cumbersome passive construction at all? If we believe language is efficient as a system, we must explain such apparent wastefulness. And we can do so only by talking about what the passive form accomplishes communicatively, how the form expresses functions that the active does not.

This contextual understanding of the passive construction has applications beyond the domain of abstract linguistic theory: It has practical relevance, for instance, in therapy. The active form of sentences is formally and functionally neutral. In the example above, the passive's meaning includes all of the active's, and, in addition, several other implications, more or less subtle: for instance, a more formal, distant relationship between speaker and hearer(s); an invitation to hearers to focus on the *ball*, the recipient of the action, rather than the actor, the *boy*, as would be normal; the suggestion that the ball represents the topic of the larger discourse, which the hearer should keep in mind. By complicating the syntax (the passive is more complex in structure than the active), passivization actually enhances understanding—at least sometimes: It tells more than the neutral active about the speaker's intentions and attitudes. At the same time, the greater syntactic complexity of the passive construction may make the meaning of the sentence harder to discern—so as much as the passive gains in interactional clarity, it may lose in pure denotative content.

Suppose a therapist notices that a client is using a disproportionate percentage of passive constructions.[2] That observation might be the basis of an interpretation, or at least a confrontative comment. The therapist's job here is first to notice constructional anomalies of this kind and to make sure that they truly are anomalous, for *this* speaker's ethnicity or gender in the therapeutic setting; then to determine their intended function (which differs from person to person: For one, it might be a means of coopting authority when feeling powerless; for another, a way to avoid responsibility; for a third, a preferred style of narrative construction). But to do this right, not merely to use a client's stylistic idiosyncrasies to undermine his or her self-confidence, the therapist must understand passivization well: its form, its functions, and their connections.

Syntax by itself is not extremely useful in understanding communication and its difficulties; but if form is seen as intrinsically intertwined with meaning and function, its significance can be great. To get a grasp on the latter two, we invoke *semantics* and *pragmatics*.

Semantics connects language with the reality, or language-external world, that it describes or creates. It is the study of the relationship between language form and meaning, or reference. When earlier we spoke of the essential equivalence between active and passive sentence pairs, we were invoking the semantic relationship of *paraphrase*, the sentence-level equivalent of word-level *synonymy*: One could replace the other with no loss in referential status. But in terms of communicative function, a question of pragmatics, there is no substitutability. Semantics also deals with the opposite, *ambiguity* (analogous to lexical *homonymy*), which occurs when a single form has multiple possible interpretations, depending on context. Both for ordinary language uses, and especially within the world of therapy, most of all psychoanalysis, these are relations of importance. We can, for instance, speak of total equivalence, complete overlap in meaning (if not communicative function): *Table* in English is *mesa* in Spanish; *it's me* is equivalent in meaning to *it is I*; in some naive theories of dream interpretation, a cigar might *always* stand for a phallus. Other semantic equivalencies are partial or specialized. A Chevrolet is a car, but a car is not necessarily a Chevrolet. A single form can represent two or more meanings, unbeknownst to the speakers arguing over them. When I say "immoral," my usage might not cover the same ethical territory as yours. One dreamer's use of a particular image (a cigar, a pearl earring) might not correspond to the same reality as another's.

People can usually count on sharing semantic systems with others who speak their language. There are always exceptions, of course, which we tend to discover once we know people well enough to get into arguments with them. Then we discover that when Al says "two o'clock," it means precisely 2:00, but when Bob says the same thing, it means somewhere in the period of time between 1:30 and 2:30. We do assume, though, that people will express their ideas clearly and unambiguously unless there is some reason not to, so that semantic unclarity—a breakdown in the link between linguistic expression and its referent—is a marked condition, requiring explanation or motivation. Just as unexpected choices in syntactic form can be explained only by recourse to a higher or more abstract level of language, semantics, so unexpected uncertainty in semantic form (ambiguity or vagueness) can be explained only by going beyond semantics, to pragmatics; likewise, semantics, bound to syntax at one end, is connected to pragmatics at the other.

Pragmaticists have tended to assume that people are efficient communicators: They accomplish what they intend to do in the best way available. At first glance this hypothesis seems starkly untenable. All around are indications that people don't, won't, or can't say what they mean, certainly not in the most direct way. Everywhere there is resort to circumlocution, prevarication, and hesitancies of every kind, all of which we have been taught to despise as inefficient use of language. Efficient communication is (we think) getting what you want to say said in the most succinct and direct manner. And we fail, all too often, to attain that goal.

Another definition of communicative efficacy states that the most efficient communication is that which accomplishes what its producer wants communicated, with the fewest untoward side effects. The communicator may or may not be fully aware of what he or she "wants" to communicate. And even the simplest linguistic utterance conveys, willy-nilly, more than one message. The trick is to settle for the form that expresses most of what is desired and least of what is not, but it is apt then to be a compromise; and, like most compromises, to be less than entirely satisfactory.

By being unclear, a speaker is saved from saying something hurtful, confrontational, or personally damaging. (We have names for this decision: Tact, politeness, defensiveness, and *savoir faire* are a few.) But the trade-off is that, by being less than utterly meaningful, speakers subject their utterances and themselves to interpretation by hearers, thereby entrusting them with considerable power. For a rational person to decide to be unclear, then, is to determine that the risks of interpretability are outweighed by those deriving from clarity.

We make these choices daily, hourly, in ordinary discourse. We tend to develop patterns, choosing one form of indirectness or another, an aspect of personal style. As long as interpretation remains possible, as long as others can discern a reason for unclarity, the choice of interpretability will be seen as rational, sometimes as preferable. But in therapy, especially psychoanalysis, interpretability and the decision to be less than clear play a more complicated role, as we shall see later.

It will be appreciated that pragmatic choices such as this are not made, or comprehended, in a vacuum, but that the context of the utterance permits its full understanding. An utterance can be very differently understood depending on where, in what tone of voice, in what communicative setting, and to whom and by whom it is spoken. This is just one subcase of the larger premise that all human behaviors are potentially ambiguous and disambiguable by context. So behavior that (for instance) is correctly taken as sexually "seductive" and legitimating a sexual response by another adult of equal status and responsibility must be seen in quite another light, deserving of a very different response, when done by a 3-year-old child, or a student, or a patient in therapy. Same act, different context: different meaning, different function, different mandated response. Failure to recognize that fact, to disambiguate appropriately, on the part of the more powerful or responsible participant, sets the stage for abusive behavior.

The foregoing is an informal treatment of a few aspects of the relationship between language form and function, for illustrative purposes. These ideas are not exclusive to linguistics or philosophy of language; they have been utilized, more or less implicitly, by various psychotherapeutic schools.[3] Instinctively good therapists make intuitive use of them—which may be why they tend not to be part of the explicit education of analytically oriented therapists. But even those therapists who have an intuitive grasp of pragmatic principles might find their thinking clarified by formal and explicit discussion. And those therapists whose abilities are not instinctive—as in many fields, probably the majority—would find the explicit presentation of theoretical concepts particularly helpful. Among those useful ideas are: conversational logic, speech act theory, and politeness theory. All contribute to our understanding of how and why people communicate indirectly; the relationship between the intended and the perceived utterance; and the various ways in which members of different groups encode their intended utterances. Understanding those ideas will clarify the working of therapy and provide ways to distinguish between cases that go well and bad examples like *Dora*, and offer reasons for one outcome or the other.

During the first half of this century, the philosophy of language, like many branches of the humanities and social sciences, was swept up in a fervor over scientific method. Leading scholars argued that, to achieve a fully rigorous "scientific" description of meaning and intention in ordinary language use, it was necessary to devise a metalanguage, a purely logical system that avoided the irrelevancies, omissions, and inconsistencies of ordinary, illogical language. But a group of philosophers, going by the name of ordinary language philosophers, argued that it was, after all, illogical to try to describe and explain ordinary language by substituting for it a system that was unlike it in highly significant and thoroughgoing ways. Yet rigor was essential for clarity.

A way out of the impasse was Grice's (1975) system of conversational logic. Grice suggested that ordinary language might be rendered sufficiently precise to produce a satisfactory descriptive system with the addition of a few basic assumptions. These are grouped under the rubric of the "Cooperative Principle," an implicit assumption guiding most interpersonal communication, to the effect that people normally wish to be understood and are capable of speaking so as to be understood, or as Grice phrased it, they can and are willing to "make [their] contribution such as is required, at the stage at which it occurs, by the accepted purpose or direction of the talk exchange in which [they] are involved" (p. 45). As a theoretical ideal, utterances will be phrased as clearly, directly, and succinctly as possible, as described by four separate Maxims of Conversation.

The Maxim of Quantity requires that a conversational contribution be framed so as to be just as informative as necessary, neither more nor less. So in response to the question, "Where is Pine Street?" (5a) will be in keeping with Quantity, while (5b) will fail as insufficiently informative, (5c) as overly so.

(5a) It's two blocks north of Main Street. Turn left at the corner.

(5b) Oh, just keep going—you can't miss it.

(5c) Well, you walk to the end of this block here. You do that by first putting out your right foot, then your left. When you get there you stand on the corner, waiting

until the traffic light is green, in case it is red, and when
it is green you step off the curb. . . .

Both (5b) and (5c) are apt to be viewed with consternation
and perhaps irritation by the recipient, who either will be bewil-
dered that the speaker isn't playing by the rules or will read in bad
intentions. On the other hand, it often happens that the Maxim is
violated more subtly, since we assume that others possess certain
kinds of information. So, for instance, even (5a) is insufficient for
an out-of-towner, but if we know our interlocutor to be a resi-
dent, we will have no hesitation in using it.

The Maxim of Quality says, Tell the truth. Out-and-out lying
is precluded, but so are irony and sarcasm, as well as hyperbole.
But as with Quantity, in appropriate circumstances, all of the
latter are both permissible and intelligible—even lying, in speci-
fied circumstances (think of the white lie, or the social fib). So the
theory must include a concept of social context, which renders
apparently unsatisfactory responses satisfactory. A competent
speaker must not only know and use the Maxims of the Cooperative Principle; but also know how and when they may (or must)
be violated, and how and when they may not.

The Maxim of Relevance requires a contribution to be relevant—that is, both to what has already occurred in the conversation and to the perceived needs of the hearer. And finally, the
Maxim of Manner requires that the necessary information be given
in the clearest, most succinct form.

Even normal utterances by cooperative and competent speakers often fail to adhere to the Maxims. The less formal the context,
the more comfortable we are with our interlocutors, the more
prior context we assume we share, the greater is the degree of
permissible deviation. Such deviations seldom cause trouble; indeed, they are often preferable to direct, fully informative choices
like (5a). That realization is captured in the second part of the
Cooperative Principle: the system of conversational implicature.

The ordinary speaker's tendency to abrogate the Maxims
makes ordinary language unusable as a logical system. But, says
Grice, if you append to the Maxims an equally explicit device
that rigorously links imperfectly informative utterances to precise
intended meanings, that problem is circumvented. That device is
conversational implicature. Grice himself never fully developed
the system, in his writings giving only sketchy examples of individual cases. Using implicature, hearers fill in what is omitted. On

the other hand, if the combination of text, context, and shared background fails to provide enough to make sense of an utterance, implicature will not rescue it: The use of implicature is based on culturally shared assumptions. So, for instance, if speakers know they are in a precarious social situation, where they are apt to be more indirect, and to violate the Maxims, they will expect implicature and will therefore be more readily able to make sense of communications that are less than perfectly lucid, like B's contribution to the bit of dialogue below.

A. Joe and Mary weren't getting along too well at dinner last night.
B. Oh, I've heard they're not doing so well in the you-know-what department, so they're seeing someone. But you know, those things take time.

With only the superficial form of B's utterance to go by, A might be stymied: On its face, it doesn't convey any content at all. But as a competent member of the culture, A can translate the vagueness into meaningfulness by the use of a lot of implicature, knowing that unusual unclarity tends to signal the presence of a tabooed topic. Since sex is among the premier taboos of polite discourse, and the context fits the interpretation, "We're talking about sexual matters," A can confidently translate B's statement into, approximately:

B'. Oh, I've heard they're having sexual difficulties. They're going to a sex therapist, but learning how to be fully sexually responsive takes time.

Far from resenting B's roundaboutness, and the extra interpretive work it makes, A is likely to feel, if anything, grateful: Not only has an awkward moment been avoided, but the very indirectness signals: "I know you share my cultural presuppositions, and will understand both why I chose an indirect route, and the meaning of the form I chose." So indirectness becomes a kind of secret handshake: *We're the same kind of people.* On the other hand, if B meant that Mary and Joe were having trouble learning to cook (since food is not currently as generally troublesome to us as is sex), it is unlikely that A would be able to draw the correct understanding.

Speakers may choose indirectness, that is, nonadherence to

the Maxims, for reasons of politeness (that is, nonconfrontation), as in this example. They may also do so in self-defense, a ploy politicians know very well. To be vague is to leave oneself room for retreat. And, as in the case above, implicature and indirectness can enhance a conversation as a subtle compliment: "I know you're smart enough to figure it out," or "I know you'll get my meaning, because we're a lot alike"; or enjoyable as an intellectually stimulating challenge.

But the understanding of indirect utterances can be problematic because members of different cultures (including different genders) have various notions, seldom made explicit, about what can be said directly and how to say things indirectly. If people living in close proximity often misunderstand each other, the relationship may not survive. Some forms of therapy (especially couple and family therapies) teach clients to recognize, more or less explicitly, their own and their significant others' ways of being indirect, and either change to be more explicit or learn to be more intuitive. What's most important, perhaps, is to learn that other people's communicative patterns are intellectual *systems*, not just craziness or ways of being obnoxious.

As with conversational logic, speech act theory arose within ordinary language philosophy out of the need for greater descriptive rigor. Many philosophers of language (in this instance, logical positivists) argued for a dichotomous definition of meaning: If a proposition could be determined to be "true" or "false," it could be said to be meaningful. A declarative sentence like (6a) could be evaluated for truth or falsity, depending on external information, and so was, in this sense, meaningful.

(6a)  The sky is blue.

But (6b) cannot be said to be either "true" or "false" as it does not provide information, but rather seeks to elicit it.

(6b)  Is the sky blue?

And (6c) is likewise not "meaningful" because it is not intended to transmit information at all, but rather to express a desire for compliance, so that truth is not an issue.

(6c)  Eat your dinner!

So in this way of thinking, declarative sentences are at least sometimes meaningful; but questions or injunctions, for example, are not. This definition exempted from meaningfulness and thus from linguistic analysis a wide array of sentence types, thereby limiting investigation to a small subset of linguistic patterns.

Austin (1962) proposed a solution by both showing that the logical positivists' solution was untenable and proposing the beginnings of a system that, while equally rigorous, was less restrictive. He noted, first of all, that declaratives came in two varieties. Sentences like (6d) can be evaluated in terms of truthfulness; those like (6e) cannot. (6d) can be questioned, or negated; (6e) cannot.

(6d)  The sky is blue.
(6e)  I apologize for laughing at you.

Austin called sentences like (6d) *constatives*, the second *performatives*. As a test for the proper use of performatives like (6e), he substituted for truthfulness the criterion of *felicity*, or appropriateness. A performative utterance was said to be felicitous if it was uttered sincerely, by the right person, under the right conditions. For instance, (6e) is a felicitous utterance just in case (a) its speaker has done something wrong ("laughing"); and (b) the wrong was done to the addressee ("at you").[4]

Austin also noticed that the force of a performative utterance could be achieved in several ways: in the case of a directive, for example, either directly and explicitly, as in (7a); directly but implicitly (7b); indirectly and explicitly, as in (7c); or indirectly and implicitly (7d).

(7a)  I order you to go to your room.
(7b)  Go to your room.
(7c)  I'd like it if you'd go to your room.
(7d)  Isn't it around your bedtime?

In (7a), (7b), and (7c), the speaker's intention is made unambiguously clear to the addressee. But (7d) is unclear and ambiguous: It might be either an indirect injunction or a direct question (a request for information). Part of the hearer's task in such cases (which are not at all infrequent) is the determination of the speaker's intention (the *illocutionary force* of the utterance, as Austin called it). But often that is difficult or impossible, especially if the context is unclear or in dispute. Thus, if both the speaker of (7d) and its hearer are in agreement that the former has the power and the authority to send the latter to bed, (7d) is quite likely to be uttered and understood the same way, as an injunction; but if the hearer disputes that claim, based on his or her perception of real-world circumstances, (7d) will not be heard as an injunction, and misunderstanding will occur. The speaker of (7d) may refer to the unsatisfactory response as "insubordination" or "disobedience," but insolence is not necessarily the reason for it.

Pragmatic theories such as those of Grice and Austin clarify the problems people face when others aren't responsive or informative in the ways they anticipate. Using these tools, therapists can teach clients to avoid problems or solve them. But therapy itself can be a fertile ground for miscommunications of these kinds if the therapist is unaware of what is happening.

Conversational logic and speech act theory deal with the choices speakers make that hearers either understand or fail to understand. Politeness theory, another branch of pragmatics, is a third perspective on these issues: whether and when to be indirect, and what form that indirectness may take. All these theories treat indirect variants as marked, requiring explanation or expansion. A cryptic utterance can be understood only by filling in (via implicature) what is omitted or unclearly stated. But markedness should not be understood as implying that indirect communication is aberrant, undesirable, or even (necessarily) less intelligible than direct.

Some cultures are more indirect than others. The Japanese, who tend to prefer indirect ways of communicating, often seem enigmatic to Americans; Americans, who prefer directness, at least in theory, seem to the Japanese overly obvious in their communication, or even childlike. Powerless people, by and large (though this statement has important exceptions), find it necessary to be less direct than the powerful. In many cultures, women's typical style of communication is less direct than men's. Some topics of discourse militate toward indirectness, as the bit of dialogue given earlier illustrates. Where indirectness is the norm or has clear justification, it will in fact be more likely to be properly understood and responded to than the direct equivalent; and indeed, in terms of both statistical likelihood and participants' expectations, will be "normal." So a skillful communicator knows whether and how to be direct and indirect, and how to translate from the latter into the former. When Freud spoke of making the unconscious conscious, as an aim of psychoanalysis, he was referring to just this sort of translation between indirect (unconscious) and direct forms of communication. People come into therapy because they dare not, or don't know how to, be direct when directness is appropriate, both between themselves and others, and within themselves. It is sometimes suggested that therapy should teach clients always to be direct. If so, it would be teaching rigid and preconceived responses to unpredictable future realities—just the sort of nonspontaneity that brings people into therapy in the first place. Rather, therapy is about learning to match form to function, content to context: the stuff of pragmatics as it is described here.

Work by Brown and Levinson (1986) and Lakoff (1978b) suggests that cultures use different systems of politeness. Indeed, a significant part of membership in a culture is knowing how to use implicit systems such as this. What was "polite" for a German in 1900 is rude for a Californian in 1990; what is polite for a Californian is rude for a New Yorker or a Japanese, and vice versa. The behavior we consider "polite" in ordinary conversation among friends is not polite, or even appropriate, in the courtroom or the therapeutic consulting room, and will be misunderstood in those places. All this is learned early in life.

As the basis of politeness theory, Brown and Levinson make use of the concept of "face," the need individuals have to seem, and feel, competent and accepted. That further breaks down into positive and negative face. Positive face includes the desire for acceptance and recognition of group membership: being liked, being understood, sharing, having feelings of warmth. Negative face includes the need for autonomy and privacy: not being imposed on, having space. Positive and negative politeness strategies address positive and negative face needs, respectively. While everyone has some need for each, cultures in their formulaic or conventional politeness patterns tend to stress one or the other. And a culture, or individual, used to framing conventional politeness as concern with negative face will misunderstand a user of conventional positive politeness as brash or intrusive; a user of conventional positive politeness will see negative politeness as cold or secretive. But both, as forms of politeness, are merely the ways a culture provides for formulaically or ritually saying, "I'm a good person, I know the rules, I won't make trouble, you can feel comfortable with me."

Adding to the confusion, a single form may be understood as

an expression of either positive or negative politeness, or as violating the rules of politeness altogether. For instance, irony may be understood as addressing positive face needs, by conveying, "We share so much as members of the same group, I can be very indirect and still be sure you'll understand"; or negative, saying, "I have something a little tricky to express, so I'll say it indirectly and leave it to you to figure it out, rather than directly confronting you with it." Or, if irony is used to someone from a culture unfamiliar with it, it may be understood as sarcasm—a form of rudeness. Indirectness can represent positive or negative politeness strategy, while directness is normally understood as addressing the positive face, or violating the negative.

Politeness systems exist to enable people to avoid threatening confrontations. Positive politeness conveys the idea that, although there may be direct confrontation, because participants are well-intentioned toward one another, the confrontation cannot be dangerous (although this may or may not actually be true); negative, that because boundaries are strictly observed, confrontation cannot occur (although this may or may not actually be true), though if it did it could be dangerous. As long as participants adhere to the same set of conventions, the system works. But if they don't, the outcome may be destructive.

Pragmatic theories explain why some communications are more satisfying and successful than others. The more unlike two individuals' strategies, the more likely it is they will misunderstand each other and communication will fail. And the greater an individual's reliance on indirect strategies for protection, the greater the chances of misunderstanding.

## NOTES

1. Some statements by major proponents of miscommunication as a causative factor in schizophrenia are found in, for example, Laing (1967), Bateson (1972), and Singer, Wynne, and Tookey (1978).

2. The obvious question is, Disproportionate according to what standard? This kind of work is responsible only when the therapist has reliable baseline figures against which to measure the client's current production: for instance, the normal percentage of passive sentences, relative to active ones, for all speakers of informal American English; or perhaps this speaker's typical percentage of passives throughout the course of the therapy, versus the percentage occurring when particularly problematic topics are broached.

To our knowledge, no such computations have ever been made, and therefore this sort of detailed work (as useful as it would be, extending of course well beyond the active–passive distinction) remains but an intriguing future prospect rather than a current reality.

One step in this direction, within psychoanalytic scholarship, is the work of Dahl, Teller, Moss, and Trujillo (1978). This paper examines the interventions of the psychoanalyst, rather than the patient, concluding that the former's use of large numbers of syntactically marked constructions (including passives) demonstrates deeper negative psychological attitudes toward the patient and her communications. It is an interesting project, and shows some recognition of the role of function in syntactic form. But their analyses (e.g., that the use of an unusual number of passives—without, it should be noted, any baseline figure—is evidence of defensiveness and hostility) do not recognize the multiplicity of possible meanings of constructions, nor do they place the sentences in the discourse context, but rather operate via a simple equation: passive = uninvolved (a sort of literal translation between two senses of "passive") = defensive. This linguistic reductionism is not surprising; it mirrors other aspects of the field's heuristic procedures.

3. Interestingly, discussion within linguistics of the multiple relationship between linguistic form and function (relations of pragmatic synonymy and homonymy) is foreshadowed by discussions in psychoanalytic literature of similar conflations of psychic organization, beginning with Freud, of *overdetermination* (Freud, 1900/1953) and *the principle of multiple function* (Waelder, 1936). As has been suggested by one of the present authors (Lakoff, 1978a), this similarity is no coincidence, but probably arises out of psychic economy: The parts of the mind are interconnected and utilize similar mechanisms. Watzlawick, Beavin, and Jackson (1967) use many of these concepts in a more explicit fashion.

4. Apologies differ from many other performative speech acts (for instance, orders or promises) in one interesting way: Sincerity is not crucially important. If someone makes an insincere promise, the recipient is apt to be indignant, since the promise is empty. But an apology exists even if the speaker is not truly sorry; and people often prefer an obviously insincere pro forma apology to none at all.

# 5

# Language in the Therapeutic Interaction

Psychotherapy is a form of communication, albeit a special form. So the therapist or teacher of potential therapists can use pragmatic principles as heuristics, sharpening the understanding of pathological communication and relating linguistic behavior to other aspects of a person's psychological and interactive functioning. Linguistic theory can also provide a tool for the analysis of disturbances in therapeutic communication, when discourse between patient and therapist is less than therapeutic. *Dora* can be seen from this point of view as an example of the kind of disturbed therapeutic communication that can be understood, and perhaps avoided, through an understanding of various aspects of communicative competence.

Linguists who work with the relation between form and function in ordinary discourse are concerned with discovering the rules of and connections among the levels of syntax, semantics, and pragmatics. The therapist involved in decoding a client's modes of expression, altering them, and using those changes to create the possibility of attitudinal and behavioral change is working with the same mechanisms. Clients (and therapists too, for that matter) may use the rules of any of these levels in idiosyncratic ways: for instance, the unusual uses of the syntactic rule of passivization described in Chapter 4, idiosyncrasies that may form the basis for interpretations. Similarly, at a semantic level, clients might use words in unusual ways, or become excessively difficult for the therapist to understand. These might suggest to a therapist a particular world view or an unusual way of looking at a situation. Or a client might (regularly or under certain conditions) display unusual pragmatic structures: for example, atypical forms of politeness, unexpected indirectness, or a style not characteristic of oral communication or unusual for that individual.

Through the medium of discourse, client and therapist work to accomplish several goals. It is significant, first of all, that language is seen in this context as *goal-directed*: Talk in therapy aims to accomplish a purpose, rather than (as in most informal conversation) being done for its own sake. For this reason, arguments that therapy is merely "paid friendship," or that friends can, in any real way, function as therapists, cannot be taken seriously.

Most obviously and simply, the therapist, by precept and example, can teach a client new communicative skills. The therapist can demonstrate how to listen; how to determine what someone else means; how to choose language for the best effect; how language is most typically used by others.

The therapeutic process (specifically the psychoanalytic model) can restore communication that has been broken or distorted within the patient's psyche; through interpretation, coherent meaning can be restored. The analyst points out where the patient's story falls apart, forcing the client to examine those points of stress and discover what lies hidden.

In these ways, therapy functions as a class in which the client learns a new language—not, of course, *in toto*, but certainly new patterns, new ways of speaking, of engaging in talk of various kinds, of understanding. The only comparable experience, for most of us, is that of learning our first language from our parents in early childhood; and, unlike second-language teaching in school, the "new language" is learned in therapy much as the first was learned: by listening and imitating, rather than by memorizing formal paradigms or engaging in artificial dialogues. The new language *must* be learned, in therapy as in childhood, if the client is to be intelligible, is to get needs met. By reinstantiating the early experience, therapeutic language learning is a significant factor in creating the transference. As with other aspects of transference, through the therapeutic experience the client will learn language again—this time, right.

And finally, the discourse of therapy restores coherency to a disturbed narrative and creates one that makes sense. By so doing, it enables the client to make sense, to self and others. The inner dialogue must be coherent if the external one is to be. With coherency, finally, comes responsibility. Rather than leaving it up to powerful others to "make sense" of them, clients learn to do it by and for themselves.

The therapeutic relationship itself constitutes a special kind of discourse, with its own syntactic, semantic, and pragmatic patterns and requirements of its own, all of which must be satisfied in order to create a "grammatical"—that is, fully functional—therapeutic experience. The language used by therapist and client is expected, on one level, to follow the ordinary rules of grammar (word formation and meaning; syntactic construction, etc.); but more abstractly, it utilizes a discourse grammar of its own: It has its own permissible conversational patterns, its own permissible sequences of topics, and so forth. It is at once language and metalanguage, since it comments on the client's use of language, and itself communicates. And as a language in its own right, therapeutic discourse is divided into levels analogous to those examined in ordinary language in Chapter 4.

The *syntax* of a psychoanalytic interview, following this analogy, is the history: on the patient's part, the *anamnesis*, the recollection of events in order, putting them in their appropriate juxtaposition. Just as with an English sentence, there is a normal order: Typically, events are catalogued as they occurred in time, sequentially. As in English, any deviation is assumed to be the product of a special and discoverable rule, enabling the true, or logical, sequence of events to be recovered. The therapist's syntactic task is that of *reconstruction*: determining what the actual sequence of events was, what has been reordered and for what reason, what has been omitted, what interpolated. And just as the syntactician working on sentences is concerned with identity relations (e.g., in *John admires himself*, *John* and *himself* refer to the same entity), therapists work with identities (e.g., the way you respond to me now is similar to the way you used, as a child, to feel about your father). These, then, are syntactic operations: They establish an order and relatedness among elements and determine what events can be said to constitute a person's history.

The *semantic* aspect of therapy lies chiefly in the work of *interpretation*: the relation between the sequence of events in the patient's life, as the patient states them, and what they mean—their symbolic functions, the way in which the patient has integrated them into a meaningful text. The semantic level of communication is the bridge between language and reality. Linguistic semantics covers both lexical and text functions: The semanticist might contrast two words that are close in meaning (e.g., *accuse* and *criticize*) and ask what they share and how they subtly differ (cf. Fillmore, 1971); or might look at a paragraph or a larger unit of discourse and ask how it coheres, what devices are used to link one part of it to the next in a seamless whole (cf. Halliday & Hasan, 1976). So too the therapist looks at individual symbols (in a dream, for instance) in terms of their meaning for the patient; or contrasts two related symbols in a series of dreams, showing how the change in symbolism signifies a change in the patient's psychological makeup; or looks at a dream as a text, seeing how its apparently disparate parts tell a single story; or comes to understand how a patient's dreams, combined with his or her symptoms, slips of the tongue, and other compromises between conscious and unconscious mechanisms constitute a cohesive narrative about the patient's perception of the universe and his or her place in it. Part of the therapist's interpretive function, then, is to encourage the patient to recast his or her symbolic system, to realign meanings and forms so that there is a better or more cohesive match between the patient's construction of reality and the real world itself. Interpretation is the "making sense" of communication, via communication. It is both communication and metacommunication—communicating about communicating.[1]

The syntax and semantics of therapeutic communication, though not under these names, have received much attention in writings on therapeutic theory and technique. But the third level, *pragmatics*, has received much less attention [and that mostly under the often deceptive rubrics of "transference" or the "working" or "therapeutic alliance" (Greenson, 1967; Zetzel, 1956)]. The dangers of overlooking this level become clear in an examination of *Dora*. Syntactically and semantically, Freud's analysis is a textbook case, whose failure cannot be accounted for. But at the pragmatic level (at which therapeutic communication not only as a way of recovering meaning for the patient, but also as a social communicative event, a linguistic negotiation involving two or more people), it is "ungrammatical"—it violates the rules of therapeutic discourse.

This claim implies that interpretation (in analytic therapy and elsewhere) is basically a form of definition—by the interpreter, of whatever is being interpreted. To define is to impart meaning or coherency or predictability to an object, that is, to contextualize it, to place it where it can function or make sense. When, as often, the interpreter's task is focused on something inanimate (a word, a text), we can say that between interpreter and interpretee there exists no interactive relationship: The interpretation will have no effect on the text itself, only on its future (animate) readers or hearers. In that sense, in that function, interpretation is apolitical, value-free, and therefore pragmatically uncomplex.[2]

But the use of interpretation in analytically oriented therapies goes beyond the understanding of inanimate text. True, this certainly plays a role: A dream is interpreted, a symptom, a slip of the tongue. And unquestionably, this use of interpretation, purely or overwhelmingly semantic, has been the focus of discussion on analytic method and theory within the research area lately designated "hermeneutics."[3] Seen in this focus, interpretation is not only an intellectually challenging exercise, but a force for good: By giving a patient's images or texts coherency, the analyst gives meaning, and thereby restores power and self-esteem (Schafer, 1983).

This understanding of interpretation as wholly benevolent and intellectual is not, however, complete. Interpreting a patient's productions is, ultimately, interpreting that patient—since one's behavior is the basis for judgments of personality. In this way, semantic interpretation becomes, in therapy, a pragmatic, interpersonal experience. In this transaction there is no semantics without pragmatics, no giving of meaning without the involvement of function. And even if, semantically, the act may be value-free or wholly salutary, pragmatically it may have a dark side. Not to recognize this is to invite serious abuse.

To provide meaning is to restore power. But to tell people what they mean is to usurp power. It is insulting to tell someone, in most circumstances, "Here's what you must mean"; it is even confrontational to say, "I don't get what you mean." To have meaning, by oneself, is to be fully communicative, human, rational; to be given meaning by another is to be placed in a lower category, as not truly a responsible language user. That is the paradox of therapeutic communication. Its justification, the therapist's superior understanding, is both what makes it work, and is the breeding ground for abuse. In the analytic process, interpretation is unilateral: The therapist makes interpretations of and to the client, not vice versa. If participants are overtly and sharply unequal (e.g., parent and child), explicit unilateral interpretability is common. Thus, a parent may explicitly interpret a child's utterance, but not vice versa. In therapeutic discourse as outside of it, people are continually faced with hard choices: whether to make interpretations, thereby achieving clarity, but risking resentment; or to leave possibly helpful clarifications unsaid, saving the other's face by avoiding confrontation.

If therapeutic communication has as one of its aims the restoration of meaningfulness to a client's words and actions, the client's choice of an interpretable communication is itself interpretable. What does it mean for the client—within the safety of the therapeutic environment—to be unclear, indirect, or disorganized? Freud spoke of this work in terms of the *Fundamental Rule*: Patients were admonished to say whatever came into their mind, without attempting to organize or polish. The analyst's job was to contrast the actual utterance with the fully intelligible variant that might, in ordinary circumstances, have been produced, and on that basis consider why the less efficient form of communication had been selected. But the therapist, too, is playing an active role, even as hearer: What does the client expect of him or her? How does the client's choice of unclear communication to the therapist reflect the client's interpersonal choices elsewhere in life?

Now it becomes clear why the majority of "neurotics" have been women. Neurosis is indirect communication. The powerless have more to gain than the powerful from indirect strategies. Women have less power than men. So, to treat neurosis (by any name) successfully, it is necessary to free the speaker of the need to be indirect. That would entail recognizing the real-world imbalance of power that creates that need, and being willing and able to empower the speaker to dispense with it. It is no wonder that virtually none of the women whose communications Freud so brilliantly interpreted seem to have been helped significantly by his method: The pragmatic component was ignored. The risk of clarity still outweighed, for them, its benefits.

Part of the danger inherent in the ability to interpret arises out of the power of interpretation to define the patient. An interpretation that, explicitly or not, leaves a patient with a loss of dignity or a negative self-image, that denies the legitimacy of the patient's distress, by mystifying the threats to dignity and self-respect arising in the patient's social context, or that otherwise restricts the patient's autonomy or range of possibilities, is damaging. The Oedipus complex, the basis of classical psychoanalytic interpretations, is just such an instance. As many feminist critics have argued, the postulation of a biological basis for the belief in feminine inferiority is a politically destructive force. The fact that these implications are expressed in terms of presuppositions that cannot be questioned or overridden as long as one wishes to be an adherent of the theory means that the patient has no access to alternative viewpoints. While in theory a patient is "free" to dispute the analyst's interpretations, the latter holds all the cards: The patient is seen as "sick," and analytically ignorant; the analyst is "healthy," and professionally trained.

Freud's original basic insight, that breakdowns in communication are the root of distress, is valuable: The parents, for whatever reason, misrepresented reality to the child, and the child, for whatever reason, distorted or closed off communication between the conscious and unconscious parts of the psyche. Both interpretive therapies and brief therapies are based on the assumption that, as unknowing and unconscious forms of bad communication cause problems, learning to undo those patterns can resolve them. Where the two types of therapies differ is in the location of the bad communication, and therefore how it is to be overcome.

Brief therapy, unlike psychoanalysis, operates in the here-and-now: Whatever prior events may have predisposed the client to obscure communication, what is relevant is that the latter is creating problems in current life, and therefore intervention consists of altering current bad habits. So the creation of myths assumes much less importance.

Interpretive therapies locate the source in early childhood: The parents create "secrets," lies, and distortions because there are things they cannot let the child know; and the child, in turn, realizes that some knowledge is intolerable, and attempts to repress it (but it is always clamoring to come to consciousness, and must be allowed to seep out, if at all, in the distorted form of symptoms and dream-symbols). The result is that the child arrives at adulthood with a sense of identity, a self-narrative, that is incoherent or inconsistent, as a narrative must be if it is to incorporate lies and distortions. The business of the therapist is, first, to demonstrate to the patient that the narrative is problematic (confrontation); second, to show the patient the reasons for the incoherencies (interpretation); and thereby, to allow the patient to develop a more rational narrative, to enable him or her to "make sense" to self and others, to allow free and undistorted communication, intrapsychic and ultimately interpersonal.

To achieve this difficult goal, the therapist must have the patient's trust, in the therapist him- or herself, and in the narrative the therapist offers in exchange for the old one. For this to be true, the therapist must offer what the patient can accept as rational and intelligent motivation for the original difficulty. That is the function of the Oedipus complex and other imaginative constructs in psychoanalytic theory and therapy.

Every belief-system that endeavors to bring its adherents to new views of themselves, and different behaviors, must rely on such foundation myths, so that the adherents can feel intellectually persuaded to new ways, rather than coerced. We can cite innumerable such myths over the millennia, each according to contemporary sources having for its followers the efficacy the Oedipus complex has for its. There are (to pick a few at random) Plato's suggested use of a "noble lie"; America's Manifest Destiny; the life of Jesus; and the Jungian collective unconscious. Each of these has demonstrated the power to induce change and loyalty among its believers.

It is important to realize that the literal reality of the Oedipus complex itself has never been conclusively demonstrated. Yes, there are plenty of anecdotal records of patients who were given Oedipal-based interpretations and subsequently improved. But all that proves is that, in a setting in which both participants have expressed a commitment to belief in the system, the founding myth of the system has efficacy. It is noteworthy that while therapy models of other types have different basic myths, all appear to work about equally well (cf. Omer & Alon, 1989; Luborsky, Singer, & Luborsky, 1975). That would suggest that it is the consensual acceptance of *a* myth, not *the* Oedipal myth per se, that does the job.

In other words, it is not the content of any particular story or myth that makes interpretations based on it "work": It is the existence and sharing of the story itself, and its acceptance as efficacious by the participants. It is ultimately the inclusion of that shared story in the cohesive narrative that the patient and therapist are building together that creates improvement: the sense of making sense—to the therapist and to oneself, and as part of a larger context—that is significant.

The majority of therapeutic theories see disturbed communication as the basis for therapeutic intervention. Analytically based models differ from others in choosing to intervene at what is perceived as the "origin" of symptoms, in early life. To justify its postulation of particular events as origins of symptoms, analytically oriented therapy must provide a reason why any particular early event was so traumatizing. The Oedipus complex provides just such a theory. But it need not be the only such causal mechanism—indeed, many others have been proposed.

Therapeutic communication, while pragmatically like ordinary communication in some ways, differs especially in its non-reciprocity. Ordinary dyadic conversation is reciprocal: On both surface and deeper levels of analysis, both (or all) parties are able to do the same things and be understood as doing the same things. But in the analytic situation, the therapist is permitted one sort of conventional behavior, the patient another. The therapist, for instance, can signal the end of the session; but if the patient should say, "It's time to stop now," it would probably not be regarded as a statement of fact, but as grist for the interpretive mill: Did the patient suddenly feel uneasy—does the patient *want* the session to be over? The patient's statement is not taken at face value, but is seen as conveying another kind of statement. Or, a question by the patient can be construed as intending to convey a declarative statement, while an identical utterance on the part of the therapist is seen as a question requiring a reply, nothing more—for instance, "How's your sex life?" Early in therapy, the uninitiated client may be prone to misunderstandings of this kind, just as the neophyte language learner makes syntactic blunders; but through precept and example, the client learns what can be said and how it will be taken.

A psychoanalyst might argue that nonreciprocity is intrinsic to the process and therefore above, or beyond, discussion or criticism. True, it is necessary; but that fact does not exempt it from examination. *Anything* specific to a form of discourse or interpersonal behavior contributes to its efficacy and its effects. The properties of psychotherapeutic discourse must be compared with those of ordinary conversation. Special rules must be evaluated: Do they contribute to function, or are they part of the field's armamentarium just because they have always been, continuing out of inertia or the need for mystification?

As with the power imbalance (to which nonreciprocity significantly contributes), the absence of reciprocity in therapeutic discourse is not to be taken as a negative attribute, or as intrinsically abusive. Reciprocity is simply a property characteristic of certain discourse types and not others. Its absence creates problems in only two circumstances: in case it is injected into ordinarily reciprocal discourse types; or if the nonreciprocity typical of a discourse type combines with power imbalance to deny the dignity or autonomy of the less powerful.

The fact that everything in discourse is inherently communicative means that any investigation of discourse meaning and function requires consideration of speakers' intentions. That in itself is problematic, since there is a continuum of *levels* of intentionality, not merely the dichotomy of its presence or absence. Beyond a rather superficial level of analysis, it is impossible to tell which, or how many, of the possible intentions underlying a specific superficial speech act are relevant. A speaker may be aware of none, or all, or several, or one; without corroborative evidence based on the speaker's later behavior, the interpreter cannot determine how accurate the speaker's judgment is. Simple cases do exist, but it is not always easy to tell whether a particular case is simple or more complex. Consider an example: At dinner, A says to B, "Please pass the salt." Without rejoinder, B hands it over. A says, "Thanks." On the face of it, this certainly looks like a simple interaction whose intentions are unambiguously patent. A needed the salt to season the food; asked for it; and received it.

But there are things we don't know about this little imaginary colloquy. Were A and B strangers? Casual acquaintances? In a committed relationship? That determination might materially affect the understanding of A's intention. In the first case, perhaps A had an ulterior motive, above and beyond the gustatory, to embark upon a relationship with B—this, too, for any of several imaginable motives. (All of this information, not discernible to the observer, is part of A's "intention" in making the request.) In the second, the request might be an opening gambit to get B's attention—again, for any of several reasons. And in the third, there is the additional possibility that the request conceals still more beneath its conventional exterior: a complaint, "You never pay attention to me"; fear, "You're flirting with the person on your right;" solicitude, "Give me the salt so you won't use it and raise your blood pressure"—these merely a few options. Without further (impossible) examination, the speech act remains ambiguous. Speakers are expected to take responsibility for their meaning or intentions only at very superficial levels. So "Here it is!" acknowledging the surface request, is an acceptable rejoinder by B to A; but, "I'm already married," or, "Okay, tell your joke," or, "I never even looked at her!" are highly aberrant, since they address hidden ulterior motives.

Much of the work in many forms of therapy focuses around the level of responsibility one or both participants can be expected to take for the less explicit intentions in their communications. Typically, the therapist's discourse is taken to be fully intentional: The therapist chose to speak as he or she spoke, and to mean it—in other words, the therapist is seen as having full responsibility for his or her actions, linguistic and otherwise. But the client's behavior is less clear-cut. While the aim of therapy is to make clients responsible for their actions, during most of the therapeutic process this ideal is assumed to be largely beyond the clients' abilities—hence the need for interpretation. And since the very fact of being in therapy implies an inability to take full responsibility for one's behavior, the therapeutic process requires the client to give over interpretive power to the therapist—that is, to assign much of the responsibility for the meaning and intent of the discourse to the therapist. The therapist must decide whether the client's discourse is intentional, unintentional, or mixed; and if unintentional, what is actually intended, and why the message was conveyed in distorted form—a role of great political, social, and psychological power, presenting pragmatic—that is, ethical—problems for the claimed therapeutic efficacy of interpretation.

As Freud (1913/1958) first pointed out, discourse, like behavior in general, does not have the same meaning in the therapeutic context as it does outside of it. So the participants in the therapeutic interaction must learn new rules: the first of the communicative changes that therapy tries to effect. But (as Freud also notes) this aspect of the therapeutic learning process is no easier than any other. Even those forms of behavior for which people are able and willing to assume full consciousness and responsibility are hard to change. And those for which they are not held accountable are particularly resistant. Among these are the rules about the form and meaning of communication, which were learned in childhood. It is true that, as people grow older and have experience with more and more kinds of discourse, they learn to modify some of the rules and expectations in keeping with new observations; but some unexamined assumptions resist change. Thus children learn at their proverbial mother's knee about behavior in the informal conversational dyad, but later, in school, they learn about floor-holding by one individual (the teacher); small children learn that questions are asked by speakers who do not know the answers, but they later learn that this is not always the case in school. Above all, people learn early and well that the most important thing is for participants in discourse to make sense to one another. To disrupt this understanding, by suggesting that another adult is failing to make sense or to be rational, is, in ordinary conversation, to commit an insult. To interpret is (by the Gricean Cooperative Principle) to suggest that interpretation is necessary, and therefore to impute to the one being interpreted a lack of rationality. People therefore will normally take the chances associated with making overt interpretations of an interlocutor's utterance only when perfect understanding is crucial, and when they would grant the other person the same right—in other words, when it is reciprocal.

Clients in therapy soon learn not to be insulted at nonreciprocal interpretation. But they cannot learn to alter the power imbalance it creates—that is automatically created by unilateral interpretation itself. By itself, this pragmatic inequality does not affect the semantics of interpretation. But there is a secondary gain for the semantics from the pragmatics. Because the continued use of unilateral interpretation serves to reinforce, in the minds of both participants, the therapist's greater rationality as well as greater power, a therapist's claims tend to become unassailable: The patient is always presumed to be wrong. So a patient cannot correct a therapist's interpretation without incurring suspicion about motives (i.e., inviting another, superordinate interpretation). It is true that psychoanalytic literature states otherwise: that the analyst should be alert to the possibility of being wrong, and that interpretation therefore should be open to correction. But not, typically, by intended and explicit verbal statements on the part of the patient (these are apt to be considered resistance); what can be taken as evidence of an incorrect interpretation is, in general, involuntary behavior on the patient's part, or at least behavior not *intended* by the patient as correction. So the only way a patient can "correct" an interpretation is via the analyst's interpretation of another piece of behavior: The power imbalance is never altered.

Those analysts who have confronted this problem argue that, while the inequity of power may be regrettable, it is inevitable— as indeed it is as long as we accept the paradigm. They tend to accept covertly another common assumption—that those with greater intellectual and social status have the unalienable right to other forms of influence over the less powerful. In this country at the present time, it is not politic to make this assumption overtly, much less to act on it explicitly (as it was in Freud's Vienna); so modern versions of analytic therapy nod in the direction of superficial egalitarianism: the use of mutual first-name address;

the tendency for both parties to sit, facing each other; sometimes, the patient's explicit "right" to question the analyst's interpretations. But the deeper and more important inequalities remain untouched, and are perhaps the more insidious for having gone underground.[4]

Even from a purely semantic perspective, the use of interpretation in insight-oriented therapy entails a covert manipulativeness that is based on, and reinforces, the power imbalance between therapist and patient. This manipulativeness rests on the nonfalsifiability of intrapsychic interpretation, linked to the principle of overdetermination. In linguistic parlance (borrowed from mathematics) a theory or rule of grammar that allows too many options in its range of applicability or its possible results is said to be "too powerful"—because of its scope, it is less than optimally precise about how language really works (cf. Chomsky, 1965). In this sense, a theory of psychic functioning that works via interpretation and invokes overdetermination is too powerful, since it provides no way to determine which of all the possible interpretations is right. In the psychoanalytic model, any interpretation or all can be right at once, and therefore there is no way to test the correctness of each: Each assumption, and therefore the whole, is unfalsifiable. Even at a semantic level, then, such a theory is basically unsatisfying as a scientific construct. But pragmatically, overdetermination renders psychoanalytic hermeneutics downright dangerous.

The pragmatic danger lies in the power given to the therapist by the excessive power of therapeutic theory—to conflate the two senses of "power." The imprecise statement of intrapsychic processes entailed in the notion of overdetermination leaves it up to the therapist, rather than the theory, to determine when a particular interpretation is valid, when to accept or reject a patient's objection. The applicability of *any* interpretive convention at any particular time or in any particular situation is determined by the therapist and only the therapist, with no possibility of achieving external validation or verification. Some commentators, such as Habermas (1971), recognizing the severity of the problem, argue that it is this very demand for *external* validation that creates the difficulty; to rescue psychoanalysis, they suggest substituting another basis for truth-judgments, for example, *intersubjectivity*—reality as determined in the conjunction of the psyches of the participants. As a theoretical construct, intersubjectivity is attractive; applied to the reality of the analytic situation, it appears not to solve the patient's dilemma or to resolve the power issue, since the patient's end of the intersubjective relation carries so much less weight in practice than the analyst's. By contrast, a linguistic theory or rule is expected to be utterly explicit in detailing the environment in which it operates, and the result of its operations: Nothing is left to the whim of the operator—the speaker or the linguist. Besides, linguistic rules are descriptive: They state how language works, not how it *should* work; and they refer to language, not to its human users. The rules of therapeutic interchange, on the other hand, have a strong *prescriptive* component, overt or otherwise, directed at human subjects: They suggest how the latter *should* speak, *should* see the world, *should* have behaved (since only the aberrant or unexpected is apt to be interpreted). Hence, these rules have the capacity to injure, and it is important to be especially careful about how they are framed and used.

So interpretation creates a serious and nonnegotiable power imbalance. It is not that this imbalance intrinsically creates a *Dora*-type (or any type) of therapeutic disaster. Rather, the semantic fuzziness (the too great power of the concept of interpretation) and the pragmatic imbalance together prevent a patient from identifying therapeutic abuse with certainty. Therapists are "too powerful": If they are competent and compassionate, there will be little likelihood of abuse; but if they fall short of the ideal, and attempt untherapeutic manipulation, unless their unprofessional behavior is gross indeed, it will not be perceptible to patients or even to knowledgeable observers. This is precisely what happened in *Dora*, except that the patient had the good intuitive sense to know she had cause to be angry, and left.[5] Rules and regulations in just societies are made to protect their weakest members. In therapy, this is the patient. If the rules of therapy do not permit patients to know unequivocally when untherapeutic behavior is occurring, then the likelihood of abuse will be great.[6]

Although therapists have developed no systematic ways of observing, much less criticizing or preventing, misuses of power through discourse, the profession does take one form of abuse seriously. Sexual relations between therapist and patient represent the most blatant misuse of the power imbalance, and one that is directly physically observable. But this is only the visible tip of the iceberg of therapeutic misuse of power. (Sexual manipulativeness is probably easier to identify than its psychological equivalent, because women have been taught not to allow men to inter-

fere with them "down there"; but they have not been taught—
rather the opposite—that they should not allow interference "up
here.") It is this attitude—it's okay if there's no sexual contact—
that gets Freud off scot-free, since he didn't, of course, lay a finger
on Dora—only, we might say, a trip. *Dora* suggests that the line
between proper and improper therapeutic intervention must be
drawn closer to the start of the continuum than it is at present.

Freud accepted as his therapeutic task to "bring [Dora] to
reason," to persuade her that her father and the Ks were not
responsible for her problems. The father referred to Dora's ideas
as "phantasies," and while Freud accepted them as *historical*
truths, he took pains to indicate to Dora (and the reader) his
contempt for mere historical, as opposed to genetic (intrapsychic), reality. What Dora claimed (he says) may well have happened, but her responses to it were neurotic. The goals of therapy
were defined by Freud in this way: Dora must become aware of
her responsibility for her predicament and on the basis of that
awareness, modify her reactions, bringing them into conformity
with the wishes of her milieu. The bizarre social situation that led
to her becoming a patient was pushed into the background, and
the examination of ongoing conflicts in Dora's family was subor-
dinated to an inspection of Dora's internal, pre-existing conflicts.

Within the analytic framework, the interpretation of unconscious, intrapsychic experience is seen as the only way to deal
with symptoms. Any attempts by a patient to define problems as
based in historical reality are dismissed as resistance, and attempts
to modify that reality directly as acting out. The goal of the therapist is to give the patient the tools with which to understand, and
thus overcome, internal conflicts. In turn, this should free the
patient to respond more effectively to threats and challenges arising from the social environment. Otherwise the therapist is expected to maintain a strict neutrality with respect to the ongoing
interpersonal life of the patient. An interpersonal understanding
of the case of Dora suggests that therapeutic neutrality is illu-
sory—there is an unstated, but real, accusation inherent in accepting a patient for individual therapy. The patient is seen as the one
with the "problem," who must be "brought to reason."

The foregoing discussion is not meant to suggest that an intrapsychic therapist is mistreating anyone who is accepted for treatment. While that case might be made for Freud's treatment of
Dora, to generalize from this to any significant proportion of the
patients seen in individual therapy would be committing an error

of the sort Becker (1964) terms "unconventional sentimentality." Becker contrasts such a bias not with objectivity, but with the dominant "conventional sentimentality." Applied to the present instance, the latter term refers to the unquestioned myths that mental health professionals hold about their work. Individual therapy is in this myth a highly ethical endeavor conducted for the good of the patient. The bulk of writing about the ethics of therapy adopts this view, and inquiry is generally framed so that contradictory evidence is ignored. Either form of "sentimental" understanding is apt to entail distortions of reality. For this reason our critique of Freud's treatment of Dora and psychoanalytic method generally is intended to note the potential for abuse—not to imply that such abuse is prevalent or unavoidable. But even if we find ourselves succumbing to the temptations of unconventional sentimentality, it may well be the lesser evil. If one outrages certain conventional assumptions by being unconventionally sentimental, a large body of public opinion will be sure to call attention to the fact and corrections will be made. But conventional sentimentality is less often attacked, and specious premises stand unchallenged (Becker, 1964, pp. 5–6).

## NOTES

1. For another perspective on interpretation, see Schafer, 1976. Actually, there are three levels of interpretability: (1) semantic, in which A = A'; analysts work at this level, as do appellate courts; (2) semantic/pragmatic, which is concerned with *why* the speaker has chosen to represent A as A' (also typical of analysts, but not jurists); and (3) purely pragmatic, concerned with what speakers gain and lose interactively by being direct or indirect, above and beyond meaning proper, and beyond conscious intentionality. (As far as we know, only linguists do this.)

2. Biblical exegesis, one example of this kind of interpretation, is apolitical purely with respect to the relation between the interpreter and the interpreted document. But the *use* made of the interpretation in the real world has political content and is not value-free.

3. See, for instance, Habermas (1971) and Grünbaum (1984) for discussion and critique of the use of interpretation in psychoanalysis.

4. Malcolm's (1984) review of Gill and Gill and Hoffman illustrates the contention that, despite superficial concessions to the appearance of egalitarianism (e.g., the Weiss-Sampson mastery-control model), abuse and misuse of interpretation are still far from unheard of in analysis. It is commendable that these innovators, members of the analytic establishment, recognize the problem and are taking steps toward ameliorating it, for instance, by allow-

ing patients to accept, reject, or amplify interpretations. But the possibility of interpretation is still unilateral, and the discourse of the consulting room nonreciprocal. Therefore analysts still have the last word—and the power, and potential to be abusive.

5. In her introduction, Kahane (Bernheimer & Kahane, 1985) takes issue with those commentators who have seen Dora's actions as "heroic":

> Although early feminist readings of the case saw only Freud's misogyny, it is too easy and ultimately unproductive . . . to point simply to Dora's victimization by Freud's overarching interpretations, to see Dora only as a resistant heroine. Felix Deutsch's description of her unhappiness and morbid anxiety cannot be readily accommodated to a vision of her victorious heroinism. (p. 25)

But Deutsch's testimony itself is biased, as more recent commentary has suggested (Goleman, 1990, citing Anthony Stadlen). His attribution to his informant of the descriptive term "repulsive" for Dora suggests the informant may not have been fully objective. Moreover, Dora's later unhappiness does not detract from her courage and clearsightedness (two concomitants of heroism) in breaking away from an abusive relationship—especially since she had no one to support her in her decision.

6. Abuse in discourse may be defined as any form of interaction that prevents the discourse from fulfilling its intended function for the participants, particularly in case the weaker member is subject to injury as a result. Thus forms of interaction that may be perfectly satisfactory in one discourse genre become abusive when they occur in another, with different power relations and different functions. So the deliberate nonpoliteness characteristic of truth-seeking genres (therapy and courtroom trials, for instance) is abusive in the classroom, which embodies analogous power discrepancies, but (although truth is involved) encouragement of learning is the function. And the win-at-all-costs forms of the adversarial courtroom are abusive in the consulting room, where the development of the weaker member's autonomy is the ultimate aim (not the discovery of truth per se).

# 6

# Communication in *Dora*

Absent from Freud's case history is any explicit analysis of the communicative aspects of the therapeutic process: the nature of the real relationship between analyst and patient, and how it contributed to the failure of the case. As Marcus (1975) and others have noted, Freud's own communicative behavior in this therapeutic endeavor was rather strange—hardly the ideal of the neutral screen he espoused, or that of warm but uninvolved concern that others might advocate.[1] Marcus and others have alluded to Freud's negative countertransference—his unconscious negative feelings toward Dora, which he appears to have neither recognized nor resolved. But most prior discussion focused on the participants' relationship as based in the unconscious of each; we want here to look at *Dora* as a conversation between two real participants who create and share a relationship in the present. That conversation, by Freud's own testimony, was not what might have been expected in a therapeutic setting of any kind, and contributed heavily to the premature demise of the analysis and, for all we know, Dora's future difficulties in life, amply attested to by Deutsch (1957).[2]

The interpersonal problems with the case fall into two major areas. First is the question of Freud's role in the family. Whose agent was he? For whose sake—in whose interests—was he "bringing Dora to reason"? A larger problem is Freud's interposition of himself into Dora's family. Rather than the analytic ideal, the uninvolved object of the transference, Freud unwittingly played, for Dora, a much more active role—one not therapeutically sanctioned. While it is true that contemporary models of couple and family therapy permit practitioners to do just that, in those the intervention is done with the full awareness of all the participants and the consent of the clients. If a therapist intervenes blindly in the family dynamic, problems can be exacerbated.

The therapeutic conversation between Dora and Freud is not, however, the only "text" the reader of the case history encounters. Nor can it be taken at face value as a "scientific" exposition of a medical procedure, an explanation of how hysteria comes about, or a statement of documented fact. At the same time, it is not "literature" in the usual sense of that term—not according to the author's stated intention, to be sure, and not according to the spirit in which many if not most readers have always approached *Dora*. In looking at the case history as a history of miscommunication and communication within and between its two participants, readers also have to consider the effect of that reading upon themselves.

*Dora* is perhaps best seen as a series of interlocking texts, each adding meaning to the others. At the same time, each re-creation of the text by a new interpreter sheds light on the purportedly historical events described—so much that, after a century of clarifying commentary, we may well be uncertain about what exactly happened between Freud and Dora. The text we are now dissecting is not, cannot be, the same one Freud produced—nor should it be taken as a literal record of Freud and Dora's conversations.

Think of the document as we now experience it as consisting of three concentric circles of text. In the center is the originating communication, the analysis proper. Surrounding it, but also infiltrating it (for Freud, in taking notes after each session, undoubtedly had literary posterity in mind) and permuting it is the secondary text—the only one with a true physical existence: the discourse between Freud and his reader that is *Dora*. This alone gives us evidence of the primary text, but it also necessarily distorts it. Also necessarily, by some of those distorting choices it creates meaning. As readers, we cannot discern the pure original conversation by itself; our understanding of it is informed by Freud's choices of style and content.

Suppose what we had, instead of *Dora*, was a faithful transcript (or better still, an audiotape) of the conversation itself: every word intact, nothing added or changed, no interpretation or qualification by Freud. Certainly it would be a precious document (not to mention the only audiotape from that period in history), but it would probably be an uninterpretable one.

Freud selected a scant few out of the huge number of conversational turns that would have occurred over 3 months of interviews, 6 days a week. He added interpretive comments, juxtaposed speech events that occurred at different times, told us how utterances were intended by the verbs he selected to report them. These choices create our understanding of the relationship between Freud and Dora. In this respect Freud the case historian blends into Freud the novelist. But even as the literary critic appreciates the affinities between Freud and Henry James, it is crucial to remember that *Dora* is in fact not fiction: Dora was a real woman (Ida Bauer was, at any rate); James is free to play with Isabel Archer, or Maisie, as his own creations, any way he wants. But how are we to solve the equation Ida = "Dora"? In this sense *Dora* is indeed a "fragment of an analysis," though not as Freud intended the title.

But even the level of discourse between Freud and his reader is not, today, our total experience of the text. The secondary and tertiary works that compose most of our bibliography themselves impose a perspective on the narrative, as the latter does to the original text. Freud's own contributions, before and after *Dora*, to our culture likewise make it impossible for us to experience his history as a contemporary reader might have been expected to. For us (as Marcus, 1975, was perhaps the first to note) *Dora* is a postmodern document, its author and narrator unreliable, its history less fact than fiction, its authority rendered dubious by the social stereotypes it left unexamined. Besides, late-twentieth-century American readers almost necessarily read into *Dora* their own therapeutic experience and/or those of friends and family, or those encountered in literature or film. In that way the modern reader is creating a text, taking that task in some measure away from its original author, reinventing it and reinvesting it with meaning.

Intention, too, shifts kaleidoscopically. The original conversation was framed as "therapy," a medical intervention whose goal was "cure." Additionally and less obviously, in undertaking to treat Dora, Freud was making a persuasive statement to his contemporaries, lay and professional: Trust me. I have a radical new method that is both explanatory and efficacious.

He failed in that intention, but the written text has as one of its functions a second attempt to achieve respectability: The text is scientific, containing *theories, hypotheses*, and *explanations*. Even if the original conversation failed in its medical goal, it could be used to provide support for another, higher one—to show psychoanalysis as a science.

Finally, many recent critics see *Dora* in still another light, as a work of literature, an artistic text to be interpreted. Like a poem—and not like a paper in a medical journal—it is not what it purports to be. Its meaning is not fully accessible.

Then if we are to understand *Dora* as discourse, we must unfold it layer by layer, from the innermost out, first assessing the original conversation, then seeing how further permutations have altered it for readers. Consider, in this regard, the language and style of Freud's original conversation with Dora—at least as well as we can experience it through the medium of *Dora*.

We will return to a closer examination of the role of Freud, as therapist, in Dora's family dynamic in Chapter 7. Here, we will concentrate on other interpersonal difficulties in the treatment: the communicative structure of the interviews as reported by Freud. Psychotherapy works mainly via the medium of language; therefore, what a patient chooses to communicate, and the form of that utterance, are properly subjected to minute scrutiny by the analyst: These observations form the basis of interpretations. (It should be noted as well that analytic discourse is even more dependent on the linguistic channel than are other forms of therapy, since so much of the patient's nonverbal communication is either distorted, entirely absent, or unavailable to the analyst's observation because of the physical positions of the participants.) But psychotherapy is not a solo performance by the client, but a dialogue in which the therapist is an active participant. This is true even in those (perhaps fictitious) versions of psychoanalysis in which the analyst says virtually nothing for hours on end. There is nothing the therapist can do, or not do, in this framework that does not constitute communication, and yet the effects of that communication—conscious or not—in this area on the development of the dialogue and the relationship between the participants remain largely unexplored territory. (Discussion of the *content* of interventions is, of course, frequent; much less so is the study of the *forms* they take, and the need to tailor these forms to the needs of individual patients.) Freud's part in the dialogue with Dora was of a highly unusual kind, whether viewed as ordinary conversation or as therapeutic discourse, both generally and in contrast with Freud's behavior with other patients, as reported by him in other case histories. The idiosyncratic nature of Freud's communication with Dora while severely damaging to the analysis and to the patient, was not merely a fluke based on quirks of Freud's personality and/or the state of psychoanalytic theory and method at the turn of the century. The problem is deeper: The errors we find in the therapist's communicative style here cannot in principle be prevented in current therapeutic interactions. Appropriate and beneficial style results from inherent qualities in the therapist, and cannot be inculcated by explicit training alone.

From the start, Freud took an adversarial position with this patient. While it is axiomatic in analytic practice that the patient's claims must always be treated with skepticism, Freud both carried his skepticism farther than usual, and allowed it to appear on the surface of his communications, rather than merely adopting it as an implicit psychological stance. There is a difference between maintaining an attitude of skepticism (holding one's credulity in reserve) and inundating the patient with accusations and assertions of disbelief. What is especially remarkable is Freud's failure to censor his responses in the written case history: His feelings for Dora and the various members of her entourage, his emotional responses to everything she had to say, come out unequivocally not only in the dialogue as he reports it, but also in the narrative portions of the case history. And if this level of emotion has been allowed to permeate a "scientific" document, written in relative tranquility and considerably after the events described, we can imagine the level of feeling that must have been transmitted to Dora during the dialogue itself.

The narrative comes to resemble less an ideal psychotherapeutic case history than the transcript of a trial in which Freud acts as prosecutor, judge, and jury, making up the law and frequently the facts as well as he proceeds. Purely in terms of the words Freud chooses to report the discourse, we see an adversarial rather than a collaborative or educational model. We are not claiming that Freud necessarily used the same words in his original discourse, though we do feel his choices in the written document accurately reflect his mood and his general intent throughout the oral conversation. In other words, the reader can take his statements as reporting, substantially, the intentions behind his utterances, intentions that were certainly conveyed to Dora by either the explicit choice of words or more subtle cues. What emerges from Freud's report is a hostility and suspiciousness that, communicated directly to Dora, must have influenced her feelings about Freud, the aims of the analysis, and herself. In therapy, as we know, different patients may benefit from very different styles of communication: One may respond best to direct statements, another to hedged questions, another to metaphors. But all patients need to be able to perceive good will in their therapists' comments, a faith in the patient's essential decency and desire for growth, a real sympathy for the patient if not approval of the patient's behavior. It is often stated that a therapist who does not feel genuine warmth for a patient will fail. We sense in Freud's report much heat but little warmth.

The words in a therapeutic discourse, like any other, mean different things depending on how they are spoken. In writing, of course, much that is available in the oral channel is gone: intonation, pitch, speed of articulation, hesitation, the length of time elapsed between one speaker's turn and the next, and so forth. But reported written narrative has ways of putting at least some of this material back in again; a writer may be more or less explicit in this way. If the narrator merely reports, in indirect discourse form, "He said that it might rain, and I felt that this was probably a correct hypothesis," a reader is likely to conclude that the reported discourse itself was unimpassioned, and also that the reporter is emotionally not very involved. But should the writer choose direct discourse, with vivid words: "He expostulated: 'It may rain!' I snorted, 'That's probably a correct hypothesis,'" the reader gets a very different picture of what occurred. Especially in a document intended to represent scientific objectivity, the imposition of an emotional stance is worthy of remark. (It is this characteristic of *Dora* as much as any other that has caused it to be likened to a novel.) If the narrator chooses to cast a great deal of the narrative in a direct-discourse format, we can hypothesize (in a true first-person narrative like *Dora*) that he is showing his own tension and excitement, particularly if the verbs of communication he uses are themselves vivid. Of course, if the writer of the case history under inspection is found to employ the same vivid format everywhere in similar works, our argument may be vitiated—the style then merely represents the writer's general psychological outlook, rather than his or her involvement in one particular case. But when we put *Dora* alongside Freud's other case histories, we find that this is not the case: Stylistically, *Dora* is unique, and therefore it is appropriate to look for an explanation for its uniqueness, and to base on this uniqueness an understanding of *Dora*'s peculiar outcome.

Freud's choice of vivid direct discourse in his narrative is all the more striking since he was writing from memory—he had no aids to jog or enliven his recollections, as a modern writer might have recourse to a tape or a transcript thereof. And if he had had recourse to a tape, we might understand the use of direct discourse more readily: It might be simply lifted off the tape, as it were. But by the time Freud was writing down the case in publishable form, he was already remote from it in time, and could not reliably claim exact memory of the words exchanged. (Freud explains that he jotted down notes about each session in the 10 minutes between its conclusion and the arrival of the next patient; but only a fragment of what actually took place in the 50-minute hour could have been recorded in 10 minutes, and only a portion of that, if any, in direct discourse.) So Freud's choice of format must be intended (always, of course, with a caution about the use of the word "intend") to convey something other, or more, than merely, "This is a faithful and exact reproduction of what actually occurred." If Freud did in fact intend to convey this idea, we must charge him with deception, intentional or otherwise, since it could not possibly be so.[3] So what can we make of Freud's choice? First, that it demonstrates unusual emotional involvement, just as it would in a novel. But also, since direct discourse intimates to the reader, "This is exactly what was said. This is just how it happened," it serves Freud as a sort of defense, an implication of historical accuracy and trustworthiness. As he would be the first to point out, going out of one's way to insist upon historical trustworthiness casts doubt on it, or at least on one's belief in it—it is "protesting too much." Certainly we can impute to Freud's decision a feeling of insecurity about some part of what he is reporting. (The historical fact that Freud wrote the case up shortly after its conclusion, then submitted it for publication but withdrew it, and allowed it to languish in a desk drawer for some 4 years lends support to these speculations.)

The use of direct discourse, in the form in which it occurs in *Dora*, gives the reader a sense of contentiousness, of struggle between the participants over who held the floor, what an utterance meant, and who got the last word (not at all the typical scenario of the ideal analytic session!). Of course it is the business of a competent and concerned therapist to be vigilant for a patient's telling gaps, omissions, errors, and other oddities in narration. But here we get the feeling that Freud took a rather peculiar relish in Dora's slips—indeed, he rejoices openly whenever he gains an inch, and delights in brandishing his formidable weapons. We find a great deal in the narrative to suggest that Freud experi-

enced Dora's analysis as a battle. For example, the words chosen
to describe the conversation remarkably often denote conflict,
opposition, and conquest (all italics are ours).

> When a patient brings forward a sound and *incontestable* train of
> argument during a psycho-analytic treatment, the physician is lia-
> ble to feel a moment's *embarrassment*, and the patient may *take
> advantage* of it by asking, "This is all perfectly correct and true,
> isn't it? What do you want to change in [it] now that I've told it
> you?" But it soon becomes evident that the patient is using
> thoughts of this kind, which the analysis cannot *attack*, for the
> purpose of *cloaking* others which are *anxious to escape* from criti-
> cism and from consciousness. (p. 35)

> Later on, when the quantity of material that had come up had made
> it impossible for her to *persist* in her *denial*, she *admitted*. . . .
> (p. 37)

> she was *obliged* to *admit*. . . . (p. 39)

> I pointed out the *contradiction* she was involved in. (p. 47)

> a fact which *I did not fail to use against her.* (p. 59)

> by *confessing that she had masturbated. Dora denied flatly.* . . .
> A further step towards the *confession.* . . . (p. 76)

> It was easy to *brush aside* this objection. (p. 101)

> And Dora *disputed the fact no further.* (p. 104)

> Dora replied in a *depreciatory* tone. (p. 105)

> She took her *revenge* on me as she wanted to take her *revenge* on
> him. (p. 119)

These are just a few examples. It should be emphasized that
the topics under discussion here, and even Freud's persistence
in ferreting out the facts, are unexceptionable: Any competent
insight-oriented therapist might find it appropriate to follow the
procedures he outlines. What is noteworthy is the *way* in which
the discourse is reported, the words chosen. For Dora, the feeling
must have been that of a defendant in court without a lawyer,
or whose court-appointed attorney is in cahoots with the prose-
cution. Everything is rejoinders, accusations, objections, dis-
putation—even when there is no evidence of argument. Freud
remarks, with no great pleasure, on Dora's fondness for argumentation. But another analyst, or Freud with another patient, might

have taken that contentiousness as proof of interest and involvement, rather than thirst for revenge. Or at least might have refrained from joining the fray.

Then there is a whole set of descriptions of Dora's behavior and character, in the analysis and (presumptively) outside of it. In all of these, Freud gives us clues that he really did not like or approve of Dora at all. We may be sure that, if this prejudice seeps into a (purportedly objective) written text, it was communicated to Dora as well.

> It was in such circumstances as these that the child had developed into a mature young woman of very independent judgment, who had grown accustomed to *laugh at the efforts of doctors*, and in the end to *renounce their help entirely*. . . . (p. 22)

> Dora was by now in the first bloom of youth—a girl of intelligent and engaging looks. But she was *a source of heavy trials* for her parents. Low spirits and an alteration in her character had now become the main features of her illness. (p. 23)

We continue to find examples of his distrust of her, eventually appearing as open dislike.

> These reproaches *recoiled* on her own head. (p. 38)

> I was quite sure she would not let herself be *deprived* of her illness so easily. (p. 42)

> . . . which gave her an opportunity for some really remarkable achievements in the direction of *intolerable behavior*. (p. 75)

And finally, there is Freud's persistence in seeing as neurotic and symptomatic (and "abnormal") behavior on Dora's part that seems to us now perfectly natural, and indeed, without alternatives for one in her position.

> Instead of the genital sensation which would certainly have been felt by a healthy [14-year-old] girl in such circumstances [being suddenly grabbed and kissed on the lips by her father's best friend, a man in his forties], Dora was overcome by the unpleasurable feeling . . . [of] disgust. (p. 29)

> A normal girl, I am inclined to think, will deal with a situation of this kind by herself. [Freud is commenting on the 16-year-old Dora's telling her parents about Herr K's proposition.] (p. 95)

In short, Dora can neither do nor say anything right; nothing
meets with Freud's approval. This is the sort of communicative
situation in which no one wants to spend time. The wonder is
that Dora endured it as long as she did. Pragmatically, expressions
of distrust and dislike are scarcely calculated to win the subject's
confidence and inspire her to be open and trusting. In fact, it
seems to us that Dora displayed unusual qualities of trust and
openness to reveal as much of herself and her internal state as she
did to a man so clearly unwilling to attempt any understanding.
Her willingness arises in part out of desperation—Freud is the last,
and only, adult in her milieu who promises any help at all. This
makes his betrayal the more poignant—and, of course, the more
damaging.

It often seems, too, that the things a therapist should be reas-
suring and understanding about are the very things Freud frames
as accusations when he suggests they play a role in her distress,
and as "admissions" and "confessions" when she speaks of
them—masturbation especially, as well as bed-wetting and sexual
knowledge. One might argue that this is just Freud's normal
couchside manner, rather than behavior specific to his interaction
with Dora, and therefore not really of interest to us. But this
interpretation is belied by comparison of this case with others.
Freud left eight detailed case histories, four (all but Breuer's
"Anna O.") in *Studies on Hysteria* (1893–95); "Little Hans" and
the "Rat Man" (both 1909); the "Wolf Man" (1914); and, more
briefly, the "Case of Female Homosexuality" (1919). Freud saw
Little Hans himself only once, and very briefly. With the other
cases, however, Freud displays a very different therapeutic manner from that which is exemplified in *Dora*. With both the Rat
Man and the Wolf Man Freud's expository style is cool and dispassionate. Both dispense very largely with dialogue, with what little
there is almost always indirect, so the reader feels much less emotional involvement. Certainly we do not have a sense of adversarial procedure, but rather, if we feel there really are two participants, we see them as two people joined together in a spirit of
scientific inquiry—much the way Freud, in his technical writings,
enjoined the reader to view the analytic process. So it seems that
with his other patients, Freud came much closer to approximating
the analytic ideal of neutrality.

For instance, in the "Rat Man," we look in vain for expressions of contention. All we find are words expressing acts of verbal education and collaboration: "I explained," "he wondered,"

"I illustrated," and the like. The Rat Man must have had an utterly different therapeutic experience from Dora's.

The difference in style seems to be due to how Freud himself felt about the analysand and the progress of the analysis. In the "Case of Female Homosexuality," although Freud expresses explicitly much of the same sorts of disapproval he felt for Dora (this woman, while attractive, was tall and sharp-featured, reasons enough for him to infer that she was "congenitally homosexual"), he speaks quite differently of the analysis itself: "The analysis went forward without any signs of resistance, the patient participating actively with her intellect, though absolutely tranquil emotionally" (Freud, 1920/1955, p. 162). While this is not the unqualified approval it perhaps superficially resembles, it bespeaks a far different experience from Dora's, one more like that of the Rat Man.

When we look back at *Studies on Hysteria*, we find Freud working to develop a style for the reporting of case histories. In general these are more impersonal than *Dora*, less so than the later cases. In the case of Frau Emmy von N., for instance, we find a fair amount of direct discourse, but virtually all of it attributed to the patient: Freud does not see himself as the actively involved participant he was with Dora. And much of the dialogue that is reported in direct discourse is treated in this way because the wording itself is of interest, reflecting Frau Emmy's obsessional symptoms: "Keep away! Don't touch me!" Freud's other case histories in this volume are much the same. Stylistically, then, *Dora* stands alone—a testament to Freud's very strong feelings about the case and the patient.[4]

With regard to other aspects of his reporting, however, all the case histories of female patients bear the marks of Freud's disapproval of their subjects—missing from the cases of the Rat Man and the Wolf Man, although at least to us, these two seem rather less attractive than the female patients. In virtually all the cases involving women, Freud comments on their unusual intelligence, articulateness, and ability to cope with what must have been highly unpleasant real-life conditions. But he seems at best ambivalent about these attributes; sometimes one gets the impression that, for Freud, intelligence and ingenuity in a woman predispose her to hysteria—probably a correct assumption, though not in the way Freud saw it. At any rate, one gets the feeling that Freud did not like being at a loss with women, resented any woman's matching him in logical acuity or verbal adroitness, and let his resentment show in one way or another. It surfaces in the case histories merely as biased descriptions; in the cases themselves, it seems to have frequently induced the premature termination of treatment, with ambivalent success at best. Conveniently, Freud's bias seems to have enabled him to avoid the problem of the erotic positive transference, which caused the unwitting Breuer such distress with Anna O. But the price Freud paid was the development of negative transference matching the countertransference, causing the precipitous ending of analyses "for revenge," Freud says, although simple frustration will explain it as well.

Indeed, if we compare Breuer's report about Anna O. with Freud's of Dora—women who, aside from the differing severity of their symptoms, had much in common—we discover startling differences. Breuer generally sees his patient in a compassionate light. Certainly Anna's behavior and symptoms must often have been disturbing and puzzling to him; certainly she was contentious, rebellious, and uncooperative as often as Dora. But he seems genuinely concerned throughout, infinitely patient, willing to put up with a great deal more in terms of extra-analytic behavior ("acting out") than Freud ever was called upon to deal with by Dora. The celebrated horror story of Anna's hysterical pregnancy at the conclusion of Breuer's treatment seems as much a result of her perception of his feelings toward her as of simple transference. And although orthodox analysis shudders at this conclusion to the case, hinting at how much better, safer, and purer Freud's analytic neutrality was, how important it is to deal objectively with the transference and not become involved, nonetheless the aftermaths of the two analyses are of interest. Both women are described by their analysts as unusually gifted. But Dora (by Felix Deutsch's testimony) retreated into an unhappy marriage, a failure to engage in any productive work, and an unending resurgence of her symptoms. Anna, on the other hand (Bertha Pappenheim, that is), recovered from her neurosis to become a dynamic force in the area of social work—a daring innovator and tireless worker, who enjoyed a full and productive life.

It is risky, of course, to venture any guess as to how their analyses might have contributed to their future lives (cf. note 2, above). But if we believe that therapy can be efficacious, we must acknowledge that their very different analytic experiences could have made a difference. Breuer, by his open support and admiration, showed his young patient that it *was* possible for her to separate herself from her destructive family, that there was opportunity and reason for trust—to use Erikson's term, fidelity—in the adult world outside. Freud, by his hostility, explicitly shut off that opportunity.

Communication is more than just words, or even the words combined into sentences. These units acquire their full meaning as entities in larger, more abstract structures, variously called *texts* or *discourses* as cover terms for a large and diverse field.

These terms (as discussed, for instance, in van Dijk, 1976) cover the range of meaningful linguistic interactions, from brief conversational interchanges to novels, courtroom trials, and psychotherapeutic treatments. They focus on language defined in terms of its communicative function. Among the requirements for a stream of connected language to constitute a "discourse" or "text" is some notion of narrative coherency: It must all hang together, whether because a single point is made, or because it all has a common aim.

Commentators on psychoanalytic discourse have recently concentrated on this form as narrative—that is, as a specific kind of discourse. Schafer (1980) has noted that the business of the analytic relationship is nothing less than the collaborative production of a narrative; Marcus (1975) and Hertz (1983) note that what brings people into analysis in the first place is disruptions in the coherency of their narrative: Neurosis itself *is* incoherency. To avoid confrontation with what would have to be encountered in a straightforward and complete narrative, patients distort their histories, formal and informal, omitting some parts, rearranging the sequence of others, distorting the relative significance of still others. That illogic allows them to go through their lives without incessant anguish, yet still feeling *enough* sense and meaning in their stories that they do not experience distress on that account—unlike outright psychotics. But they do lose the thread, and have fears on two grounds: either that what has been so carefully hidden will yet surface; or that everyone will know that, as rational creatures, they are shams.

The work of the analyst is that of an editor, or perhaps a philologist restoring an ancient manuscript: adding, deleting, rearranging to produce a more lucid text or restore its original form. This view makes the work of analysis clearly collaborative. The patient supplies the raw material, but the analyst makes it work as a text.

Outside of psychotherapy, we tend to think of our life stories as purely our own product. They are evidence of our identity.

Only we can evaluate them as "true" or "false." But in the therapeutic process the picture changes. What a client represents as
"truth" or "history" early on may later be supplanted entirely or
greatly altered in a new version. (Erikson's 1962 discussion of
reality and actuality is germane here.) A successful analysis, the
production of "less and less distorted derivatives," should have
as one end product a single, cohesive, fully intelligible narrative
subscribed to by both its creators. But how is this to be achieved?
If at any point in the analysis patient and analyst differ—as collaborators in any creative venture are bound to do—whose vision
will prevail? How will compromises be made?

The resolution of this conflict is the test of the analyst's skill,
delicacy and fairness. Above all, true collaboration must be main-
tained, or the power imbalance will assert itself abusively and the
function of therapy, the achievement of autonomy, will fail. If
the analyst assumes responsibility for the production or understanding of the patient's narrative, it will cease to belong to the
patient, and the latter's dependency on the analyst to "make
sense" will be heightened. Yet, since this is collaborative work,
the analyst has something valuable to add to the construction.

Some discourse types involve a nonreciprocally produced
narrative (e.g., a novel: the writer produces it, and the reader
makes sense of it); some, like conversation, are reciprocal (all
participants do the same things, speak or listen). Some narratives,
like those produced in therapy, are collaborative in that they are
the result of both parties working together to produce a single
text; others, like a trial, are adversarial, with the job of the defense
being the destruction of the narrative produced by the other side.

We have noted the resemblances between some of Freud's
talking to Dora and one side's treatment of the other's witnesses
in a trial. It is not surprising then that the narrative in *Dora* has
affinities with a trial transcript. Dora produces her narrative,
which Freud treats with skepticism, sometimes to the point of
substituting his own. By ignoring the requirement of collaboration, Freud effectively subverts the treatment and coopts Dora's
role as coproducer of the narrative. Rather than helping her learn
to be responsible for her own coherent narrative, he denies her
access to her own story, confusing her understanding of reality
and disrupting the adolescent task of building a viable adult identity. Freud fails Dora doubly: He denies her own perceptions, thus
interfering with the formation of identity; and he denies her a
true collaborative role in the construction of her narrative. In so

doing, he reduces her to dependency on him, and later others: Only they can tell Dora who she is; she has not learned how to do it; she has not achieved autonomy.

The "text" of the analysis is not merely the conversation between analyst and analysand. The communications of each of them with others in the analysand's milieu also figure into it. Then how did Freud's interactions with the members of Dora's circle influence the course of the analysis? Freud considered his acquaintance with both Dora's father and Herr K, and his conversations about Dora with the former, to be harmless. But were they? By allying himself as thoroughly as he did with Dora's father, Freud effectively established himself in her mind as someone she could not trust. And since he was the last, as well as the most authoritative, of a series of adults who had betrayed her trust, Dora could hardly help taking from her brief analysis the message that no adult, and particularly no man, could be trusted.

The extent to which Freud's identification with Dora's father (as well as Herr K) is made manifest in his communication with her is extraordinary (e.g., in the passage from page 23 cited above). Dora's father hands her over to Freud with the words, "Please try and bring her to reason" (p. 26). In the next paragraph Freud, as if echoing her father, refers to Dora's "impossible behaviour" and later (p. 75), her "really intolerable behaviour." Indeed, the anamnesis itself is given not by the patient, but her father, and Freud accepts his version with only minor quibbling; Dora must enter the treatment as seen in the light of her father's prejudiced testimony, and her father often seems to be speaking through Freud. Freud certainly does accept it as his therapeutic task to "bring her to reason," which, as defined by her father, means to persuade her that her father and the Ks are not responsible for her problems. The father refers to Dora's ideas as "phantasies," and while Freud accepts them as historical truths, he is at pains to indicate to Dora that while what she says happened may have happened, her responses to it were and are unrealistic. Hearing this, Dora had to place Freud in her father's camp. So the function and intent of the analytic discourse are perceived very differently by the two participants. Dora is engaging in it to please her father on the one hand, and on the other as a last desperate attempt to find an adult to trust and be trusted by. Freud fails her by seeing the conversation as a means of "bringing her to reason," that is, reconciling her with her family on *their* terms. When two participants in a discourse see it so differently, it can only fail.

Freud's fusion of his aims and understanding with those of Dora's father is continually, and strikingly, in evidence. It seems rather unusual for a physician, seeing a patient with "low spirits and an alteration in . . . character," to concern himself first of all with the difficulties these made for her parents—or rather, her father. In fact, Freud gives us much evidence that her father is the person he is working for, not Dora, and her father (who is, after all, paying the bills) is the member of the family Freud most respects—or better, the only one he respects. It is true that Freud comes to agree with Dora about her father's motives; but the agreement is grudging and hardly complete. He still feels that Dora's mere historical truth is unimportant, and thus denies her the full satisfaction of being really right. And while the passage on page 23 is about the only one in which anything favorable is said about Dora at all, there are many admiring references to her father: He is described as "a man of rather unusual activity and talents, a large manufacturer in very comfortable circumstances" (p. 18). Freud remarks upon the father's "shrewdness" (p. 23) and "perspicacity" (p. 24) despite the latter's rather extraordinary blindness (not the sort caused by a detached retina), enabling Herr K to send the 16-year-old Dora, living at home, flowers every day for a year without arousing the "shrewd" man's suspicions.

So Freud is acting as Dora's father's agent, and Dora's antagonist.[5] When a therapist identifies the purpose of therapy in terms of the needs of someone other than the patient—that is, acts as someone other than the patient's agent—the whole concept of therapy becomes dangerously distorted. If the purpose of therapy is to help the patient feel more comfortable in life and achieve autonomy, then a therapist acting on instructions from someone else will seriously compromise these aims. In such a case, the therapist—more or less consciously—will tend to perceive the patient's health in terms of how well the patient's behavior meets the requirements of that other person, rather than how well it works for the patient. Since most often (very clearly in this case) psychological distress arises out of a mismatch between the patient's needs and what those in the patient's environment want from him or her, a therapist who acts as the agent of anyone other than the patient is doing something untherapeutic. It is not at all an exaggeration to call it a betrayal.

Spence (1986) discusses a number of problems inherent in the psychoanalytic case history as a textual genre, some of which have been discussed in Chapter 5. But *Dora*'s problems in this respect go beyond that of the ordinary case history—another reason why the case has aroused extraordinary interest.

Spence discusses several confusions in psychoanalytic case histories as texts: Are they intended to affect their reader as (scientific) *explanation* or (humanistic) *interpretation*? Science represents itself as fully explicit and clear; humanistic discourse, the stuff of literature, delights in uncertainty and ambiguity—the more so since Freud himself gave us reason to see ourselves that way. The aim of scientific communication is the imparting of information. True, scientific texts have persuasion as a secondary goal, but they achieve that end by presenting *proofs* that the entire community can concur with and accept.

In literary texts, persuasion assumes a larger and different role. Here the writer's explicit aim is *interpretation*. Interpreters must rely on their own psychological processes; additionally, for their efforts at winning the reader over to succeed, their implicit assumptions must match the reader's to some degree. These assumptions, unlike the shared beliefs of the scientific community, are typically not consciously held, nor need they be explicitly demonstrated, nor need their truthfulness be proven; plausibility supplants falsifiability as a requirement. The process by which humanistic persuasion occurs is private—each reader for him- or herself—rather than utilizing, like science, the physically accessible data available to all. Therefore persuasiveness assumes a more critical role, and form supersedes content in significance.

Scientific discourse, while of course read by individuals separately, is addressed to readers in their public, or institutional, roles as scientists; imaginative literature, on the other hand, appeals to readers' private and unique understandings and experiences. Scientific text speaks for the communal *we*: This is what we have demonstrated, what we believe. The addressee is likewise a collective entity: If English had a distinctly plural second-person pronoun, it would be used. Literature is discourse between *I* and (singular) *you*. Hence the much maligned tendency of scientific prose to use the first-person plural and impersonal modes of expression has a rationale. (Indeed, the frequent aridity of scientific prose may be functional as well, demonstrating the intent of its producer to inform, not to entertain.)

Sociolinguists have discussed the differences in form and function between private and public discourse (cf. Bernstein, 1962; Gumperz, 1982). To summarize some of their findings, public discourse must be intelligible to any member of the larger community; private discourse is just for an intimate few. So the communication of the public sphere uses the standard language, attempts especial clarity, avoids idiosyncratic usages; it tends to be direct and explicit. Private language, on the other hand, is supposed to be indirect, allusive, and idiosyncratic: Those choices convey, "Only people like you and me can understand this. We are the same kind. We can trust each other."

Psychotherapeutic discourse is particularly private. A scientific treatise, both as publication and as science, is highly public. But the psychoanalytic case history confounds the two. It is at once informative/scientific, and aesthetic/literary. It offers explanation in the form of interpretation; it is private, in representing private discourse, and public. It attempts to satisfy the conditions of two genres. But often they operate at cross-purposes, and to the degree that they do, the workings of the case history can be abusive. It often (*Dora* is an especially striking case) offers interpretation in lieu of publicly demonstrable evidence. While the private, idiosyncratic grammar of the narrative collaboration produced by the participants in the analysis is appropriate to that singularly private setting, it is uncertain how it translates into the public discourse of the case history, and how interpretation turns into explanation.

Other problems of genre assignment present themselves. A scientific text—and Freud's explanatory stance and scientific language identify *Dora* as intended to belong to this category—requires at least an appearance of factuality and objectivity. But problems arise in both these spheres. We have already noted the ambiguities between "fact" and "fiction" in the text. Even if we assign *Dora* to the former category, are we to further assign it to the realm of hard science, or philosophical speculation? Freud seems to want to couple the prestige of science with the relaxed evidentiary requirements of philosophy. The models of Copernican astronomy or Newtonian physics assume an uninvolved, objective observer standing apart from the subject under investigation as an essential part of scientific method.

More recently, philosophers of science (as well as post-Newtonian physicists) have become aware that even in the "hard" or physical sciences pure objectivity and uninvolvement are at best an unattainable ideal, and perhaps an obstacle to understanding. The observer, by the very act of observing, becomes a participant: There *is* no true objectivity. Scientists are human: They desire fame and fortune; they like to be right. Even the most hard-nosed scientific research is not immune from subjectivity, of both legitimate and illegitimate kinds. The problem is only compounded by the insistence that science and scientists *must* be objective—when in fact they cannot be so.

The difficulty is infinitely greater for the social sciences—the metaphorical nature of whose name is too infrequently appreciated. If even subatomic particles are in some sense responsive to an investigator's presence, how can the mind of another human being be immune? Any honest investigator—whether in psychology, anthropology, sociology, or linguistics—must admit that there are interactions between subjects and investigators that may, unbeknownst to the latter, affect results: No one can be fully objective, and one's subjectivity trickles through the veneer of uninvolvement. This is even more the case in the analytic situation, where a patient, via the transference, becomes inordinately dependent on, and sensitized to, an analyst's subtlest responses. On top of this, the patient's behavior is not presented in the literature as raw data, but through the analyst's interpreting eyes. And the analyst, writing the case history, undoubtedly has a theoretical position to defend. So it is incredible that analysts claim that their interpretations of patients' utterances constitute objective science. Far better for the field to part company with "science," redefining itself as "art" akin to that of the literary critic, or "faith" like that of the ministry.

It can be argued with much justice that the tangles in which psychoanalytic discourse finds itself (specifically the self-contradictions Spence discusses) arise from a misunderstanding of science. It becomes clearer all the time that the strict dichotomies that seem prerequisite for taxonomization and rule construction in the early stages of a scientific discipline (linguistics comes immediately to mind) are, with later sophistication, seen to be oversimplifications, necessary at the early stage, but later to be discarded if progress is to be made. Science was once seen as requiring discrete, dichotomous categorizations: An entity is either $A$ or not-$A$; light consists of particles or waves, not both. But with greater sophistication has come the understanding that dichotomies are false clarifications. Light is both particle and wave. Observed and observer fuse. Even more clearly in the social sciences, reality is more accurately captured in terms of partial identities, or continua. A lexical item like *categorization* may exhibit the properties of both a noun and a verb; in saying, "People can get in trouble that way," a speaker can at the same time intend to utter a threat, give advice, and make a declarative statement (and probably other possibilities). Human beings are free to indulge in the psychological comfort of dichotomization; the real world, unfortunately for our self-possession, does not operate that way. But psychoanalysis, insecure like the other social sciences, abhors imprecisions of this kind, and much prefers to assign behavior to rigid dichotomous categories: conscious or unconscious; neurotic or normal.

By this reasoning, Dora must either "know" or "not know" about adult sexual behavior and terminology. Freud, discovering that she has seen books on sex, assigns her to Category *A*, as a sexually sophisticated adult woman with an adult's sexual responsiveness, since the only other available dichotomous category is not-*A*, or "innocent child." This conclusion enables Freud first to assault Dora with sexual innuendo and implication, as he might an adult woman (if he dared); and second to decide that the 14-year-old Dora should have been sexually responsive to and compliant with Herr K's advances.

But it makes more sense to say that Dora's sexual capacity fell into a fuzzy category, neither *A* nor not-*A*. She had some knowledge, in the form of passive "book learning," mere terminology; but she lacked experience and full maturity, "street smarts." There is, as Freud remarks elsewhere, knowledge and knowledge. So both Freud and Herr K are sexually assaulting someone who is an innocent child in important, if not all, respects, because both deny the possibility of fuzzy categories. For them, if Dora knows *anything*, she knows *everything*. Logicians refer to this as *pars pro toto* reasoning, a logical fallacy.

As a text, *Dora* offers the richness of a tapestry, the ambiguities of a palimpsest. It exists on many levels. At each, confusion about intention and function are grounds for misunderstanding and abuse. The dialogue between Freud and Dora, the analysis proper, veers between therapeutic and punitive, collaborative and adversarial. The discourse between Freud and his reader is ambiguous as to genre: literature or science? Finally, the text as we read it now both is and is not the text Freud offered to the public in 1905: His own contributions to our thinking about human nature mean that we today understand *Dora* not as he and his contemporaries did—and yet, we can see the original reality only through his eyes. These confusions make for a text that is intellectually and ethically disturbing, and yet (or therefore) continually fascinating.

# NOTES

1. The ideal of analytic neutrality, the "blank screen," like most important constructs of psychoanalytic theory, has been subject to some rethinking since it was first proposed by Freud (1913/1958). Its earliest form was very strict: The analyst was to become as invisible as possible to the patient, to display no emotions or beliefs; have no interactions whatever with the patient outside the work of the analysis itself; refuse to gratify the patient's libido, literally or symbolically; not exchange gifts, favors, and so on. The reason, of course, was to protect the purity of the transference. Anything the patient was permitted to discern about the analyst's real life or personality would both interfere with the former's projection on the latter of the characteristics of those in the patient's own life; and make it harder for the analyst to reliably identify *any* attribution of traits by the patient to the analyst as manifestations of transference.

Later it was recognized that the model Freud suggested was impossible to attain, and in fact not even fully desirable: The analyst had to permit some responses and attitudes to be discernible, to provide the patient with a model of appropriate ways of behaving. Nevertheless, despite these modifications, the sort of allowances Freud made with Dora would surely not be countenanced by any modern psychoanalyst or analytically oriented therapist.

2. A question that can probably never be answered is: What responsibility does Freud have for Dora's later unhappy life? The question can be explored from several points.

First, as noted in Chapter 5, note 5, it is unclear how much credence should be given to Deutsch's testimony. Second, supposing Deutsch's report is accurate, we cannot overlook the possibility that the real world, rather than intrapsychic conflict, was the primary source of Dora's malaise. Some marriages are unhappy; some children disappoint. And life in post-World War I, pre-Nazi Germany could not have been conducive to robust psychological health, for a Jewish woman with Socialist relatives. Finally, even supposing Deutsch's report to be correct and Dora's unhappiness internally generated, it is unclear whether that unhappiness was merely the result of her earlier life, with the analysis playing *no* part; or whether Freud's mismanagement actively contributed materially to the outcome.

We cannot know; but we can say with some certainty that had Dora improved, Freud would surely have claimed credit for that. In fact he did, prematurely, in the final paragraph of *Dora*.

Years have again gone by since her visit. In the meantime the girl has married, and indeed—unless all the signs mislead me—she has married the young man who came into her associations at the beginning of the analysis of the second dream [actually not correct]. Just as the first dream represented her turning away from the man

98                                                               Father Knows Best

she loved to her father—that is to say, her flight from life into
disease—so the second dream announced that she was about to
tear herself free from her father and had been reclaimed once more
by the realities of life. (Freud, 1905/1953, p. 122)

If the analyst may freely take credit for work well done, should he not also
take the blame when later evidence indicates a bad outcome?

3. Modern pragmaticists and sociolinguists are correctly suspicious of
data derived from any source but exact recording of the discourse itself,
for example, in conversation, through audiotapes. Recollections, even notes
made immediately following a conversation, do not constitute reliable evidence. In fact, contrary to our intuitive beliefs, it has been shown (Loftus,
1979) that the more emotionally charged an interaction, the less accurately
it will be remembered.

4. Hertz (1983) comments insightfully on Freud's stylistic peculiarities
in *Dora*, arguing that they demonstrate intrapsychic peculiarities of Freud's
own. He likens Freud's omissions, falsifications, circumlocutions, and exaggerations to the incompletenesses, inconsistencies, and hyperbole characteristic of hysterical communication (cf. Shapiro, 1965). By these techniques, he
suggests, Freud is unconsciously identifying with his patient. We see Freud's
stylistic anomalies from an interactional perspective: What is Freud saying
to Dora? To the reader? Why?

5. By his own implicit testimony, Freud goes well beyond acting on
behalf of Dora's father. In numerous ways he actually *becomes* the man,
achieving an identification between them. He cannot then be a neutral, objective observer of the family dynamic.

The identification is not surprising. For "ein vermogender Mann," Herr
K had much that Freud, in 1900, would have desired: economic security,
professional success, status, sexual freedom. So Freud's subtle equations are
significant: The two men are about the same age, of roughly the same social
stratum, both "passionate smokers," an odd phrase to be sure. Freud describes Herr K (and thinks of himself) as "shrewd" and "perspicacious."

# 7

# The Interpersonal Framework:
# An Alternative Model

Traditional interpretations of *Dora* have focused on the patient's hysteria, its roots in her infantile sexuality and resultant character development, and the skill with which Freud uncovered these factors in his treatment. Inquiry has been directed to the nature of her condition and the exploration of its structure and genesis. It is generally conceded that Dora was involved in an odd and distressing set of interpersonal relationships, but these more contemporaneous influences tend to be relegated to the background. Our discussion, however, re-examines Dora's condition in the context of these relationships; her symptoms are seen as part of a larger interpersonal system. Our particular interest is in how these relationships influenced her in becoming a patient, and how the structure of the therapeutic relationship in turn tended to influence the future interactional patterns in her life. We examine these relationships as the theater for conflicts that traditionally have been located in Dora's psyche.

Our understanding of *Dora* provides an alternative to a psychoanalytic perspective on the case. However, we are not attempting to evaluate the verifiability of psychoanalytic theory or the effectiveness of psychoanalytic therapy. Rather, we are concerned with the interpersonal context of Dora's patienthood and the pragmatic implications of the way treatment is structured in such a system. Thus, we are less concerned with the correctness of particular psychoanalytic interpretations than with their impact on the patient's relationships.

From an interactional perspective, it can be argued that intrapsychically oriented therapeutic approaches have a peculiar insensitivity to the social forces that lead one person to become a patient and not another. Like Dora, many people live in a set of unpleasant relationships, and the distress from which they seek relief arises in the context of these relationships. What is generally ignored, however, is that "the ability to identify behavior as problematic and a person as a patient is not evenly distributed within social systems" (Coyne & Widiger, 1979). A person's identification as a candidate for therapy may well reflect the efforts of more powerful members of the environment to localize a systematic problem within one individual and to convince this person to accept the responsibility for change.

Freud was aware of Dora's family circumstances and described the family's intrigues and concealments with remarkable clarity. He also acknowledged that Dora had not herself sought treatment for her multiplicity of hysterical symptoms, but rather "it was only her father's authority which had induced her to come to the treatment at all" (Freud, 1905/1953, p. 22). Adolescents commonly enter treatment under pressure from their parents, and although this can create predictable difficulties, their solution is generally seen in technical rather than ethical terms. We, however, are interested in exploring the social context of Dora's patienthood in a way that highlights the ethical complexities of treating adolescent patients in particular, but also individual therapy patients in general.

One way to understand the interpersonal circumstances of Dora's symptoms and patienthood is in terms of Glaser and Strauss's (1964) concept of an *awareness context*, the "total combination of what each interactant knows about the identity of the other and his own identity in the eyes of the other." The relations between Dora's parents and the Ks can be characterized as a well-choreographed *mutual pretense*. All four were strongly committed to preserving the appearance that each marriage was intact and that Dora's father and Frau K had a platonic relationship, even while fully aware that the contrary was true. "In some sense everyone was conspiring to conceal what was going on, and in some yet further sense everyone was conspiring to deny that anything was going on at all" (Marcus, 1975, p. 253).

Besides identification of the interpersonal system as one of mutual pretense, application of an awareness context paradigm requires that we establish (a) the structural context under which the awareness context exists; (b) the consequent interactions; (c) the changes in interaction that occasion transformations of the context (such as Dora's father's feigning illness in order to vacation with Frau K); (d) the tactics of various interactants as they attempt to manage changes of the awareness context; and (e) the consequences of the awareness context and its transformations for the interactants. Specifically, we are concerned with the demands that maintenance of the mutual pretense make on Dora, how her symptoms express these demands, and how her patienthood strengthens the pretense.

It took considerable coordination of effort for the two couples to sustain the pretense over an extended time period. Actual and feigned illness served to legitimize the basic structure of the relationships among the four adults: the lack of involvement within the two marriages and the closeness of Frau K and Dora's father. Situations inevitably arose that threatened to expose the couples' shared fiction, and the changes in routine required by illness were used to convert them into innocuous events. Thus, complaints of physical illness allowed Dora's father to disguise his trips with Frau K, and Frau K's complaints prevented Herr K from forcing the issue of a lack of sexual involvement in their marriage.

The estrangement of Dora's parents was tied at least in part to Dora's father's having contracted syphilis before marriage and subsequently infecting his wife. This was an enduring source of resentment for her and led to her continued avoidance of sexual activity with him. When he became ill with tuberculosis, his need for care and his wife's withdrawal provided the excuse for Frau K to assume the role of nurse, and for him and Frau K to take bedrooms near each other and away from their spouses.

Prior to assuming responsibility for attending to Dora's father, Frau K had spent time in a sanatorium for "nervous disorders." She had been unable to walk for a time, but as a nurse became "healthy and lively." This remarkable improvement as well as her positive impact on Dora's father became a sufficient justification for the time they spent together.

Herr K was frequently away on business trips. Upon his return his wife would complain of ill health and take to her bed, even though she had been healthy before his arrival. According to Freud, she detested sexual relations with her husband and sought to avoid them with a regularity that Dora noticed.

Dora's father blatantly used complaints of deteriorating health to justify the trips in which he would be joined by Frau K.

He would complain about the climate, cough, and declare that he must leave for the town of B_____ because of his condition. Once there he would write cheerful letters home. Dora was able to discover that Frau K's travel coincided with his, and concluded that they must be having a rendezvous.

It would appear that Herr K and Dora's mother derived the least benefit from sustaining the pretense. Initially Herr K's questioning and protests posed a problem. He complained to Dora's mother, but there is no indication that he received any support from her. He also pressed Frau K for a divorce, but when she stopped using the children as an excuse for refusing one, he dropped the issue. Freud suggested that he was freed by the affair to pursue his own romantic interests. The lack of at least an appearance of a stable marriage and family life may have made his sexual pursuits more obvious.

Freud rejected the notion that Dora's father formally handed her over to Herr K to silence him, but did acknowledge an implicit understanding that Herr K could pursue Dora if he did not interfere in his wife's affair. Herr K had to suffer a number of indignities, including his wife's feigned illnesses, her lack of sexual availability to him, as well as the affair, and he was the major threat to the preservation of the arrangements that had been worked out. A sexual relationship between himself and Dora would have restored equilibrium to the system. However, once he had failed in his seduction of Dora, and was exposed by her, he had as much to gain by invalidating her perceptions as did anyone else and dutifully played a role in protecting the system against her attacks.

Dora's mother is the least developed of the four adults. Freud knew her husband quite well, but had never met her. Based on the reports of Dora and her father, Freud characterized her as a foolish and uncultivated woman who had retreated into her housework and whose obsessive concern with cleanliness made home life miserable for the rest of the family. Apparently she became hostile and troublesome to her husband when she first learned she had contracted syphilis from him. She shared an unconscious alliance with Dora, who believed that as his daughter she would suffer from the disease as well. Freud noted that Dora "identified herself with her mother by means of slight symptoms and peculiarities of manner, which gave her an opportunity for some really remarkable achievements in the direction of intolerable behaviour" (p. 75). Yet consciously Dora despised her mother.

By the time of Dora's treatment, the mother's hostility was

much less overt: By then she must have felt utterly defeated. Perhaps it was because of this that she lost the support of Dora. Her daughter now "looked down on her . . . used to criticize her mercilessly and she had withdrawn from her influence" (p. 20). Dora's mother might be able to salvage a modicum of dignity as long as her plight was not made explicit and if the status of her relationship with her husband was not apparent to the outside world.

Although Freud presents the mother as weak, unobservant, withdrawn, and foolish, her willingness to deal with threats to her marriage was unambiguous. She met a number of challenges from Herr K, Dora's governess, and Dora. She resisted Herr K's complaints as well as the urgings of the governess, who insisted it was beneath her dignity to tolerate the affair. After her husband and Frau K moved to adjoining bedrooms, Dora complained to him, and he replied that his children should be grateful to Frau K. When Dora pressed her mother for an explanation of this, the mother invented a story about how Frau K had saved Dora's father from suicide. Dora knew that this was implausible: Her mother was covering something up.

Despite their animosities and diverse motives, the four adults found common cause in sustaining their intricate system. While their awareness of the pretense is clear, Dora's understanding of it is more ambiguous. At first she showed a remarkable insensitivity to indications of what was going on, and she rejected the governess' attempts to alert her. "She drew Dora's attention to all the obvious features of their relations. But her efforts were in vain. Dora remained devoted to Frau K and would hear of nothing that might make her think ill of her relations with her father" (p. 36). But later, just prior to therapy, Dora had become an excellent detective, exposing Frau K and her father's clandestine meetings and sexual activities.

At least some of our difficulties in evaluating what Dora must have known and how hard she must have worked to avoid knowing stem from Freud's confused presentation of her stage of development. As previous writers (Glenn, 1978; Marcus, 1975) have noted, Freud at various times refers to Dora as a "girl" and a "child," yet assumes that she possesses the understanding and sexual responsiveness of a mature woman. Freud rationalized Dora's father's lack of alarm at Herr K's attentions by saying, "Dora was still a child and was treated as a child by K" (p. 35). Yet he could argue that it was pathological (i.e., hysterical) for the prepubertal Dora to react with disgust to Herr K's advances; that is, he assumed a fully adult responsiveness.

Dora benefited considerably from the closeness of the two families, at least initially, and she may well have accepted her growing awareness of the adults' arrangements so long as they did not require her to behave inappropriately. She was very much attached to the Ks, took care of their children, served as confidante and advisor to Frau K, and received presents from Herr K. Nevertheless, maintenance of the pretense made numerous demands on her. She had to move with her family and tend her father when he complained of ill health. Later she even helped orchestrate afternoon visits between Frau K and her father. She avoided the Ks's house when she believed her father was there, and kept the children with her out of the house at those times.

In Chapter 2 we summarized the two incidents between Dora and Herr K, the first in his place of business when she was 14, the second beside the lake when she was 16. In between, Herr K frequently gave her expensive presents, and sent her flowers every day for a year. Although her father could hardly remain ignorant of this behavior, he did nothing about it. Further, when Dora reported the second incident to her mother, and she to Dora's father, and he confronted Herr K, who denied it, the father turned on Dora. And still more, Herr K's excuse to Dora's father was that Dora had been reading sex books—an excuse patently handed to him by her confidante, Frau K.

Interestingly, Dora's hostility was directed not toward Frau K, but toward her father, whom she accused of handing her over to Herr K so that he would better tolerate the affair. Dora demanded that her father break off all relations with the K family, but as he told Freud,

> that I cannot do. For to begin with, I myself believe that Dora's
> tale of the man's immoral suggestions is a phantasy that has forced
> its way into her mind; and besides, I am bound to Frau K by ties of
> honourable friendship and I do not wish to cause her pain. (p. 26)

When Dora revealed that Herr K had propositioned her, the response of the Ks and her father indicated that the three were willing to turn on her to protect their own arrangements. The interpretation by Dora's father upheld the pretense: He had only an "honorable" relationship with Frau K, the Ks loved Dora dearly, and it was only in the pathological fantasies of a young girl obsessed with sex that things could appear otherwise. The fundamental reality of Dora's experience was thus sacrificed.

If we accept it as a sincere demand, Dora's ultimatum to her father appears quixotic. Yet an alternative interpretation is that at least in interactional terms, its most important feature was that it forced an explication of Dora's role in the pretense. The father now had to acknowledge that the relationship with Frau K was more important than Dora's claims on him. With this explicit, Dora could distance herself from the machinations of these adults. The cost was high: She relinquished her illusion that she was valued for herself and not for her role in their game. Yet it was a cost already paid, for they would not have allowed circumstances to progress to the attempted seduction if they valued her otherwise. Dora obtained an acknowledgment of her devalued status, but it came in the context of a concerted effort to invalidate her experience. Her symptoms can be viewed as a response to this, a redoubled effort to comment on her role in the system and resolve the pretense.

Dora lacked dramatic hysterical symptoms like Anna O.'s. Besides her shortness of breath, nervous cough, loss of voice, and migraine headaches, she had fainting spells and had written a suicide note. Yet it was her ongoing depression, irritability, and hostile attacks on he parents that made life most difficult for them.

> Low spirits and an alteration in her character had become the main features of her illness. She was clearly satisfied neither with herself nor with her family; her attitude toward her father was unfriendly, and she was on very bad terms with her mother who was bent on drawing her back into taking a share in the work of the house. (p. 23)

Dora also exposed her father's use of physical complaints, accused him of malingering, and uncovered the fact that he and Frau K had left town at the same time. Dora further charged that her father was insincere, thought only of his own enjoyment, and tended to see things in a self-serving way. Freud indicated that he could not in general dispute these accusations. He took issue only with her charge that there was an explicit bargain between her father and Herr K concerning her availability.

From an interactional perspective, it is significant that symptoms frequently appear when a person confronts an impossible situation and attempts to break out (Haley, 1973). However, the emphasis is less on the initial emergence of the symptoms than on how they persist, becoming interwoven and concatenated with the response of others (Coyne, 1976; Sluzki, 1981). In *Dora* Freud notes that the factors that maintain symptoms may be quite independent of etiology. A symptom may come as an "unwelcome guest" (p. 43) yet acquire a secondary function that anchors it in the patient's life. In the absence of this, "it may vanish . . . easily, apparently of its own accord, under the influence of time" (p. 43). Freud goes on to indicate that a secondary function can probably be found in all fully developed cases, and for Dora the aim was clearly

> to detach her father from Frau K. She had been unable to achieve this by prayer or arguments; perhaps she hoped to succeed by frightening her father (there was her farewell letter) or by awakening his pity (there were her fainting fits); or if all this was in vain, at least she would be taking revenge on him. . . . She knew very well . . . how much he was attached to her, and that he asked after her health. (p. 42)

In the context of the pretense, Dora's symptoms became a biting commentary on the behavior of the adults, a parody of their tactics for maintaining the arrangements. Freud noted that there was an exaggerated quality to her distress, a lack of seriousness to her suicide note, and an important way in which her charges that her father was malingering also applied to her. Yet, focused on establishing the relationship between symptoms and intrapsychic conflicts, Freud gave little attention to the significance of the symptoms for their interactional context.

Dora's suicide note may have been a ploy, but for the four adults to label it as such risked further comment on the father's alleged suicidal moment in which he was saved by Frau K. Likewise, her physical complaints invite the label of malingering, but reflect on the use of physical complaints by the adults.

Accounting for the exaggerated quality of Dora's behavior, Freud detected an underlying *tu quoque* (Latin for "you too") structure to it. Thus, her reproaches against her father for malingering had a "lining" or "backing" of self-reproach. Within an interactional framework this *tu quoque* quality is evidence for the relationship between her behavior and that of the significant people in her environment. Dora was trapped in their well-choreographed system and was being sacrificed. Protests brought no relief, but only a concerted effort to invalidate her perceptions. She accepted her role, mimicking the behavior of the adults, pretending in a manner that embarrassed their pretense and threatened to bring it down.

Within an intrapsychic framework, on the other hand, a *tu quoque* quality in behavior simply identifies it as sick ("projection"), and further, it becomes important evidence in locating responsibility in the patient for her predicament. She is rebelling not against the adults, but rather she is a conflicted woman in rebellion against herself, someone needing insight: Her choice of symptoms is read as a confession of responsibility for her predicament.

Freud acknowledged that a change in Dora's social circumstances would have alleviated her symptoms. "I am quite convinced that she would recover at once if only her father were to tell her that he had sacrificed Frau K for her health" (p. 42). However, as we noted, it is not appropriate for a psychodynamic therapist to intervene directly in the patient's environment. Even to suggest or rehearse strategies for dealing directly with environmental difficulties is moving out of analytic neutrality, contaminating the transference, and therefore countertherapeutic. But Freud went beyond therapeutic neutrality: He took the moral position that it would be wrong for the father to accede in any way to Dora's demands. To do so would reward her symptomatic behavior. Dora faced an overwhelming environment in which the four adults most important to her lied, pretended, malingered, and made demands on her that showed little concern for her well-being. Dora's symptoms certainly contained elements of pretense and malingering, and as a patient, she bore in her analyst's eyes a special moral responsibility. The legitimacy of her demands on her environment was dismissed; she had resorted to symptoms and become a patient, and this became the moral issue, not what was being done to her: Having resorted to indirect, symptomatic communication, at least in Freud's eyes, she relinquished any moral claim on the adults in her life.

Freud conceded that her recovery might depend on changes in circumstances, and that her symptoms might otherwise persist. There too he resorted to the language of moral condemnation: "Yet if her father refused to give way to her, I was quite sure she would not let herself *be deprived of* [italics added] her illness so easily" (p. 42).

Freud afterward expressed uncertainty as to what Dora

wanted from him: "I do not know what kind of help she wanted from me" (p. 122). As various writers (Erikson, 1962; Langs, 1976) have noted, it is likely that Dora wanted Freud to intervene with her father or at least hoped that Freud would acknowledge that her perceptions, invalidated as they were by the adults, were nonetheless correct. Freud did neither, and by invoking the language of genetic versus historical reality, provided further invalidation of Dora's position.

What would have been a just and possible outcome for Dora? Freud argued to Dora that Herr K had a "perfectly serious plan" to divorce his wife and marry her, a plan in no way "impracticable" (p. 108). If only Dora had let Herr K finish his proposition, it might have ended in a proposal of marriage. In the closing pages of the case history, Freud mused on whether it would have been better for Herr K not to have accepted Dora's slap as signifying a final "no." Freud pondered whether there would have been "a triumph of the girl's affection for him over all her internal difficulties" (p. 109f). The moral verdict and the sentencing were complete. Dora was guilty and should give in to the demands being made on her.

Suppose Dora (and Herr K) had acted in accordance with Freud's ideal scenario: Herr K persisting in his "proposal" despite Dora's slap; Dora hearing him out and being persuaded; their marrying and living, Freud trusts, happily ever after. Freud felt this outcome might well have brought Dora permanent symptomatic relief, based on his intrapsychic reasoning. Her unconscious wish for Herr K would now become psychologically and socially acceptable, able to be consciously acknowledged and acted upon. The communicative link between conscious and unconscious would be reforged, with no need any longer for distortion, so the symptoms would vanish. Intrapsychically, the marriage would be just what the doctor ordered.

But looked at interpersonally, the outcome might have been less idyllic. Herr K, after all, was still married to Frau K—Dora's friend and confidante. Could Dora have turned her back on Frau K and her children, betrayed her without a twinge of remorse? Frau K's acquiring her freedom (much less desirable for a woman at the turn of the century) would itself have upset the adults' mutual pretense system. Frau K would very likely have begun to pressure Dora's father to divorce his wife and marry her. Dora's mother would be far more directly threatened. And Dora would be blamed as the instigator of the trouble. She would become estranged from her family and her closest friend, forced to depend on the understanding of Herr K—whose previous behavior had not shown him as a man of great empathy. It seems unlikely, from this perspective, that Dora's symptoms would have gone into permanent remission. She would still have plenty of need for them.

The conventionally sentimental view (Becker, 1964) is that psychodynamic therapy is a form of treatment that the patient initiates to relieve emotional distress and that, by liberating the patient from internal conflicts, renders him or her better able to cope with internal and environmental demands. Ignored are the large number of instances in which more powerful members of the environment coerce a person into accepting therapy in order to increase his or her conformity or to delegitimize demands on a situation. Acknowledgment of such pressures raises complex ethical questions, potentially requiring a restructuring or refocusing of therapeutic efforts.

In the last of his *Introductory Lectures on Psycho-Analysis* (1916–17/1963), Freud stated that while the patient's current circumstances and surroundings have little theoretical interest, they were of the utmost practical importance. He attributed many of the failures of psychoanalysis to situations in which members of the social environment put their own interests before the patient's recovery. In such instances, "we had in fact undertaken something which, in the prevailing circumstances, was unrealizable" (Freud, 1916–17/1963, p. 459). When the influx of patients became too large, he attempted to deal with the problem by excluding anyone who was not "*sui juris*, not dependent on anyone else in the essential relations of his life" (p. 460). This odd and impracticable solution has generally been ignored. Instead, therapists have persisted in an ethical stance appropriate only to the rare and perhaps even mythical *sui juris* patient.

Freud's discussion—such as it is—presupposes that the typical patient enters and remains in therapy voluntarily. This presumption is necessary if the therapist is not to view his or her job as analogous to that of a slave-owner or prison warden. And clearly the noninstitutionalized, noncourt-mandated patient is not in a position realistically analogous to a slave or convict. Yet such a person is not often (if ever) fully "free," and his or her entrance into and remaining in therapy are not truly 100 percent voluntary. Dora, for instance, entered therapy at her father's behest, defined as "sick" by her father, upon whom she was emotionally as well as financially dependent. She was not, then, in therapy "voluntarily.'' Yet she considered herself free to leave, and did so when she chose to, without (as far as we know) feeling any need for her father's advice or consent, and without (also as far as we know) incurring thereby any ill effects. Or consider the members of a couple or family who enter therapy as a unit: Most often the other(s) are there because of the insistence of one member—most often, the one who is the most powerful. In general, unless patients enter therapy for their own sake, not because of advice or urging from others (however subtle), and feel free to leave, therapy cannot be considered voluntary, and therapists must, to some degree, see themselves as complicit in a more or less coercive relationship.

# 8

# Dora as Female Patient

Dora's symptoms can be understood as a way of dealing, however inadequately, with a milieu that imposed overwhelming demands on her, and from which there seemed to Dora no plausible means of escape. In turn, the family milieu confronts and colludes with the larger social milieu. Had Dora been older—or a man—or perhaps a young woman of very unusual initiative, she might have found a solution through some means other than *petite hystérie*. But for a not altogether extraordinary woman in turn-of-the-century Viennese society, bound to her family by ties of affection and economics, her education and training inadequate and her preconceptions (and those of her society) opposed to her finding a way of earning a living on her own, her symptoms were probably her only escape, or at least her only permissible cry for help. A contemporary therapist encountering someone in Dora's position would be expected to appreciate and be sympathetic to her dilemma. While Freud cannot reasonably be held to a contemporary standard, it is still legitimate to ask about the cost to Dora, and to us today, of Freud's shortsightedness. How did Freud's inability to empathize with women contribute to the breakdown of communication between him and his female patients, and to the failure of this case and the tragedy of the remainder of Dora's life? To what extent, finally, are Freud's difficulties with Dora symptomatic of difficulties intrinsic to psychoanalytic therapy as long as the therapist is male, the patient female?

There has been much discussion of Freud's views on feminine psychology in the literature of the feminist movement and elsewhere.[1] It is generally agreed that Freud's thinking about women, as well as his treatment of them, was affected by unconscious bias—a bias he seeks, in several of his writings, to deny, but which colors all his work in this area. We need not recapitulate here the evidence that has been presented that, in *Dora* as elsewhere in his writings, Freud acted as an apologist for the Victorian patriarchal family and the society that supported it, and was supported by it; that with Dora, as in his theorizing about infantile "seduction" (cf. Masson, 1983) and the Oedipus complex, he repeatedly over-looked or undervalued clear evidence that the female patient was at the mercy, sexually and otherwise, of the male members of her family; and that this exploitative relationship was at the heart of the symptoms presented by so many of these women.

Alongside (or as an adjunct of) feminist critique, there have been a number of attempts, from several perspectives, to effect a rapprochement between feminism and psychoanalysis, or create a "feminist psychoanalysis": Consider especially the influential work of Mitchell (1974) and Chodorow (1978). But these coura-geous attempts seem to us less than totally successful, perhaps because there *is* no logical combination of intrapsychic and soci-etal explanations, or at least any such attempt must be far more explicit about recognizing the provenance and effects of each, separately as well as together, where they may be synergistic.

It is helpful to recognize, with these authors, that psychoana-lytic theory contributes to the understanding of gender develop-ment and differences, an understanding that must underlie any feminist reinterpretation of gender-based roles and stereotypes. Chodorow argues persuasively that the mother's personality and mothering style are of crucial significance from very early in the child's development. In this her contribution differs from the Freudian viewpoint, which sees the father as the major force af-fecting the child's (of both sexes) sexual and characterological development, the mother serving mainly as a kind of inanimate object whose possession can be fought over by father and son, or whose failure to supply the female child with a penis can be re-sented. But reinterpretations of this kind, however necessary, are not sufficient to rescue the classical theory from its intrinsic sex-ism, since Oedipal resolution continues to lurk in the underbrush.

Writers such as Mitchell and Chodorow, who have attempted a rapprochement between feminism and psychoanalysis, need to downplay the centrality of the father-dominated Oedipal crisis in female psychosocial development, one way or another. To believe in the biological reality and theoretical centrality of the Oedipus complex was, for Freud, "bedrock": the basis upon which followers were accepted into the fold or cast out, like Adler and Jung early on, Horney and Reich later. Modern analytic theorists have tried to incorporate these dissidents into the fold. While their openmindedness is salutary for the field, their proposed changes in theory create confusion in their attempt to conciliate feminism (as they wish to do for political, economic, and/or occasionally philosophical reasons). To hold a belief in the literal reality of the Oedipus complex while providing a satisfyingly cohesive intellectual basis for a theory is to disavow the equality of male and female. In the first place, it downgrades the importance of the mother in a child's development; secondly, virtually all developmental issues revolve around the possession, or not, of a penis: who has one, who has lost one, who is likely to lose his, with consequent contempt for anyone who doesn't have one. To accept Oedipal theory is to agree with Freud (1931/1961), (1925/1961), (1924/1961) that the possession of a physical penis, by biological necessity, makes one a superior human being because the threat of castration induces in the male child the development of the marks of higher civilization (namely, a conscience and the ability to sublimate). It follows then that one who, being female and castrated at birth, need not fear castration has no strong impetus to acquire these characteristics. As a consequence women's conscience and capacity for sublimation are (as a result of biological or anatomical inevitability) weaker than those of men.[2] And a woman who tries to be like a man, to acquire male conscience and ability to be creative (sublimate), does not thereby become higher or better. She demonstrates a neurotic symptom, "penis envy," difficult to eradicate by psychoanalysis but necessary to overcome to achieve health and sexual fulfillment.[3] It would seem then that attempts to create a "feminist psychoanalysis" are wishful thinking, predicated upon the ability to ignore conflicts at several levels between the theories. If it's feminist, it's not psychoanalytic; if psychoanalytic, in any meaningful sense, not feminist.

Freud saw the sexual issues in therapy as revolving around physical (genital) sexuality and its repression or expression in the transference. Indeed, his interpretation of the failure of *Dora* is that he did not interpret the transference (he indicates that he means the positive erotic transference) early or strongly enough. Dora had fallen in love with him as representative of her father (whom she had loved Oedipally) and Herr K, whom—according to Freud—she had desired and wished to marry, himself a stand-in for her father. But more important both in the development of

Dora's illness and in her breaking off the analysis is a different gender relationship: the exploitation of power by the male and its use to protect the societal status quo. When a therapist is male and his patient female, like Freud and Dora, the power differential of the consulting room is buttressed by, and in turn contributes to, the male/female power imbalance of society as a whole. Power in the therapeutic relationship, as we have said, arises out of the therapist's role as unilateral interpreter. Not irrelevant is the fact that in ordinary life men implicitly take for themselves the right to interpret women and their behavior unilaterally. While a man's communicative actions (tone of voice, words, bodily stance and gestures, etc.) need have no meaning besides what is intended, a woman's behavior very often does, in men's eyes: For a man to touch a casual female acquaintance or even a stranger, to stand close to her in conversation, to wear revealing clothing, is merely to be friendly or fatherly, or to be expressive in one's dress; for a woman to do the same with a man in an analogous relationship is too often construed as "asking for it"—that is, issuing a sexual invitation. A woman who does none of these, on the other hand, is not understood as merely not making such a statement, but is interpreted as making a negative statement: "I don't want to have sex with you," and therefore being unwomanly, unnatural. She cannot be neutral, and her behavior, in whatever form, can always be construed in terms of its serviceability to male needs. This attitude is so pervasive that most of us have ceased even to be consciously aware of it; but it colors our behavior and sense of ourselves. Certainly it illustrates the contention that interpretation is the right the powerful have over the less powerful, as well as a means by which the powerful assert and reaffirm their power. And of course, it is seen most clearly in *Dora*, where Freud—departing from his usual awareness of the ambiguity of all behavior—again and again reduces all Dora's symptoms, all her statements, to the sexual: Their meaning is desire for her father, Herr K, or Freud himself, or the homosexual absence of that desire. Only in their reference to three men at once, not in the possibility of having other than sexual import, are they overdetermined. Freud has often been accused by his critics of reductionism, turning all human motives into sexuality; but less apparent is the relationship between this tendency and the preponderance of women patients in his practice. Freud's precept, "when a patient says no, she means yes," and so forth, is not unrelated to the male presumption that when a woman says no to sexual advances, she means yes—a common rationalization of rape. Both are justified and allowed to occur by power imbalances. Both take from a woman the right to speak for herself, to define her own meaning.

Not only does Freud rely on the implicit power imbalance between male and female, therapist and patient, to guarantee his right to make interpretations and insist they be taken seriously (anything else is "resistance," and there is no analogous term to describe a therapist's refusal to comprehend the patient's communication, as happened between Freud and Dora). He "overpowers" Dora, as we have seen, by the anger of his communication with her (the explicit expression of anger, traditionally reserved for men, is a good way to reinforce personal power over others), as contrasted with the reports of his dialogues with male patients: He argues, he browbeats, he shames, he lectures; he doesn't explain, or illustrate, or explore. It is Freud-versus-Dora; Freud-along-with-the Rat Man. With his male patients, Freud takes pleasure in their intelligence: It makes the job of explanation easier, makes their communication more stimulating. But with women—with the *Case of Female Homosexuality* and Freud's cases in the *Studies on Hysteria* as well as *Dora*—the intelligence of the women is commented on with impatience or outright exasperation, or at best amused tolerance. Intelligence in the inferior member is not conducive to hierarchical power relationships, and gets in the way of unilateral interpretation; on the other hand, in a more nearly egalitarian relationship, it enhances the experience of both participants.

Of particular interest in our understanding of the communicative debacle that was *Dora* is an examination of the way in which the analyst's power is created, utilized, and enhanced within the special conditions of the consulting room and the particular situation of the male analyst–female patient. Here, as elsewhere, communicative strategies create and reinforce power relations and assumptions about power. The argument can be made with reference to individuals or groups; and involving any kind of discourse in which power must be determined, or allocated, or utilized. Most relevant to our interests here is the power differential between men and women generally and its exemplification and exacerbation through the forms of communication characteristic of each.

Language represents reality but also creates it. If one person speaks hesitantly and one forcefully, one indirectly and one directly, observers will ordinarily assume that the power of the latter (in terms of the ability to get desired things done) is greater than that of the former. And if, through this differential use of language, the latter's aims should be accomplished and the former's should fail, that outcome would likely serve to convince observers and participants alike that the latter deserves to be the more powerful of the two, enhancing and legitimizing the imbalance still further (cf. Erickson, Lind, Johnson, & O'Barr, 1978).

A considerable body of empirical research suggests that, in most societies that have been studied in any detail, there are modes of communication stereotypically assigned to and expected of men and women. Women are supposed to represent themselves as indecisive, indirect, and deferential; men, as forthright, direct, and authoritative. This is not to claim that real discourse always follows these prescriptions; but in general we feel more comfortable the more closely we approximate the ideal appropriate to our gender, and our interlocutors do likewise (see Tannen, 1990).

Women's conventional deference takes many explicit forms. Women are expected to be interruptable by men, and not vice versa. Men tend to choose the topics of cross-gender discussion. Women use more markers of uncertainty and hesitancy, as well as more forms suggesting that their addressee determine the meaning of their utterances (cf. Lakoff, 1990, for some discussion). In short, women's conventional communicative styles form a pattern consonant with, and interpretable as, powerlessness and unclarity. But it is important not to translate this conventional appearance automatically into a real desire to be powerless, or an inability to express oneself clearly enough to merit being taken seriously.

While linguistic habits of these kinds are learned in childhood and ingrained in time, they can be changed with determination and understanding. Unchanged, linguistic habits represent a force for conservatism, providing rationalizations for mistreatment and discouraging the speaker from perceiving herself in new ways. The first step in changing linguistic patterns is to analyze one's communicative effectiveness. Psychotherapy can be a potent force in bringing about such changes—as long as it is not used to represent conservative interests that argue for predetermined roles and the status quo, perhaps on the grounds that the way men and women communicate is "natural" and "normal," or that, since it has always been so, it should (or must) always be so. A therapist who bases judgments of psychological health on stereotypes and tradition in this way is untherapeutic and is acting, in every such case, not as the agent of the patient, but as the agent and representative of a repressive society.

It would be comforting to state that therapists are, and have always been, too sensitive and too intelligent to fall into this "adjustment" and "normality" trap. But research such as that by Broverman and her associates (1970), with more recent confirmation in Hare-Mustin (1983), contradicts that comfortable hypothesis. Broverman and associates demonstrate that therapists do not see the ideal "healthy" woman as active or independent. Those are traits ascribed to "healthy" human beings by the therapists the Broverman team surveyed, and to "healthy" men as well—but not to "healthy" women, who were expected to display the opposite traits. A therapist taking such a position would, in guiding a female patient to psychological "health," not encourage the development of those traits, as he or she would in a man. And if this attitude was present in therapists in the United States as late as the mid-1980s (even if more subtly manifested by then), it is not surprising that it existed in a practitioner in turn-of-the-century Vienna. But the theoretical and methodological armamentarium of psychoanalysis goes even further in underlining and legitimizing the communicative power imbalance between men and women—and therefore the power imbalance in general.

We have spoken already of the power implicit in the use of unilateral interpretation. To be interpretable, a communication must be indirect—must not say directly what it intends. Powerlessness both leads to and requires indirectness and the disguising of communicative intent (because the powerless have the most to lose by a communication that is unpleasant to the one in power). Women thus utilize indirect strategies for two reasons: first, because they *are* in fact often powerless and dependent, and would risk real retribution if they were to be direct; and second, because women are trained to *appear* powerless as a form of "femininity." If psychogenic symptoms (such as Dora's) can be read as indirect communications of ideas that are too dangerous to be uttered directly (and this must be the assumption if they are to be dealt with via interpretation), it makes sense that it is the powerless who are most prone to develop such symptoms, and we understand more clearly the oft-cited statistic that the majority of people who seek psychotherapy are women. (This is only one reason, actually: Another is that—as with Dora—in a family situation in which there is a high general level of dissatisfaction, the weakest member tends to become the "identified patient," the one whose "sickness" is keeping everyone else from being completely happy; once she is "brought to reason," everyone feels, everything will be all right. Similarly, family and marriage are still often thought of as the business of the wife or mother; so if something goes wrong in those spheres, it's her fault, and her responsibility to fix it.)

For all his astuteness in recognizing hysteria as an expression of disturbed communication, Freud failed to explore the question fully. With our current awareness of the relationships between language form, social status, gender, and power, we can reevaluate Dora's development of symptoms as a rational, if unconscious, choice—given her options. For the preferred symptoms of hysteria, those that recur in case histories, including *Dora*, all represent exaggerations, ironic commentaries and sarcastic rejoinders on their sufferers' society's perception of women's minds and roles.

Irony and hyperbole are indirect ways of communicating, among those referred to in the discussion on indirectness in Chapter 4. The Cooperative Principle states that we understand one another as intending to make sense (that is, as speaking with reference to the Maxims of Conversation); but that when, as often, there is deviation from those principles, we utilize rules of conversational implicature to determine what was actually meant, provided we can understand a reason for deviation from the discourse context. The Maxim of Quality requires speakers to be truthful, that is, to say only what they know to be true. This proviso obviously excludes outright lies, but also hyperbole, understatement, sarcasm, and irony, all of which superficially make claims the speaker knows to be false. But since we utilize most of these devices with the expectation that the hearer has enough additional information to know what we really intend to convey, implicature generally is safely used to achieve full comprehension. (Lying is an exception: We resort to it precisely when our interlocutors cannot be expected to know that we are being untruthful, with the aim of creating misunderstanding—the very antithesis of the Cooperative Principle.) Under these conditions, irony and analogous devices function as both protection for the speaker (since the communication is indirect) and subtle flattery for the hearer (since their very indirectness suggests that the speaker sees the hearer as intelligent and as a member of the group). But all these devices, to be fully communicative, require a hearer willing and able to process the indirectness: In avoiding the risk of confrontation, they entail the risk of misunderstanding.

The aberrant communicative strategies of hysteria can be described as violations of the Maxims of Quantity or Relevance—that is, as evasive and beside the point—as well as Quality. But Quality violations seem, more than the others, to be used to make veiled statements about the relation between a speaker and other participants in the discourse. This is just what the hysteric is doing.

The hysteric's symptom-statements are ironic exaggerations of the Victorian ideal female stereotype. They say, in effect: "You want me to be sickly, passive, and dependent? Watch me—I'll do it better than you believed possible—and you'll be sorry!" For, carried to hyperbolic heights, stereotypical female modes of behavior *are* inconvenient and irritating to those who hold power. (And if their inherent sarcasm is perceived, even subliminally, by those who want to "help" the hysteric, the anger such patients arouse begins to make perfect sense.) Nor is it surprising that hysteria so often afflicts the intelligent and ambitious woman of the period: She has the brains to see the unsatisfactoriness of her situation, the impossibility of a happy solution; and to devise a way out that apparently adheres to society's dictates, yet rebels against them, throwing the expectations and demands of society's powerful back in their teeth. But, because these are expressed as "symptoms"—the unintentional reflexes of "illness"—those at whom they are directed *cannot* react punitively, but must realize, at least, their inconveniencing power, if not (consciously) their hidden sarcasm and subversive intent.

Dora's symptoms, seen as ironic communications, fulfill their purpose admirably. The aphonia: "I cannot speak: I am a woman, I have no say. So I will say nothing." The malaise (or *taedium vitae*): "I am inactive, uninvolved, because I am unable to take the initiative." The stomach pains: "I am in pain, in the very region that defines me as a woman, and I need to be taken care of." And the suicide gesture: "I'm just a woman—maybe I shouldn't be allowed to live."

Both Freud and we see the symptoms of hysteria as indirect communication, used when direct forms are too threatening. But Freud saw the issue as *sexual*: For him, what women dared not express was their need for sexual gratification. We, on the other hand, see the inexpressible thoughts as *political* in nature: the relationship between men and women in a patriarchal society.

The former, while certainly threatening to the entrenched power structure, is nowhere near as threatening as the latter. The former, after all, merely legitimizes men's sexual use of women, while the latter, properly understood, demands a complete re-evaluation of sexual politics.

Then Freud's treatment of hysteria was doomed to failure (hence the lack of success in his case histories). The aim of psychoanalysis might be said to be to give the patient back her voice, enable her to communicate directly rather than symptomatically. Freud saw the analyst's task as essentially that of the language teacher: teach the patient to recognize and interpret the utterances of the unconscious, the id; to translate them into the language of the ego. But the conduit can be fully and permanently undammed only if there is no need for further damming. The patient must be freed from fear of the consequences (intrapsychic and interpersonal) of direct, intentional communication. Freud taught his patients that sexual desires may be safely communicated and so effected partial "cures." But the need for autonomy and self-realization could not yet be communicated, so the barriers remained in place.

Now we can understand better what happened to Dora under Freud's ministrations. While Freud with every interpretation encourages Dora to become aware of her sexual feelings, points out their reflexes in her dreams and associations, and finally blames the premature termination of the analysis on his failure to take certain sexual aspects of the therapeutic relationship into account, he ignores the at least equally potent force of another repressed emotion—anger. Dora certainly had enough reasons to be angry, but she could not express these directly to those she was dependent upon; if she did, she would be ignored or punished. As a dutiful Victorian daughter, she probably could not articulate her anger fully even to herself. Here is the basis for all sorts of symptom-formation—the suicide note being just the final *denouement*. But Freud, while acknowledging that she certainly *was* angry—at him, at her father, at her mother, at the Ks—interprets the anger as that of "a woman scorned" in love, rather than a person whose autonomy is systematically being denied. Half a loaf is unarguably better than none, and getting sexuality unrepressed is surely worthwhile; but it is foolish to pretend that it is the whole loaf.

Manifest throughout is Freud's lack of sympathy for women, his tendency to see them purely in terms of their services to or difficulties for men, his inability to empathize with them as full human beings. To Freud, a woman is relevant principally in terms of her sexual capacities. Her behavior is sexual or nonsexual, but never asexual (that is, determined by other needs and interests). Hence, the only explanation for Dora's anger toward various men or disgust when she is accosted is that there is unconscious sexual motivation (desire or resentment at rejection) behind it. Additionally, any emotional feelings a woman has must be sexual, first and foremost. A man can feel friendship for other men, or anger toward them, without, for Freud, the necessary imputation of homosexual motives. But Freud seems unable to believe that one woman's emotional response to another can be anything but homosexual—that is, erotic and perverse. Let us grant a sexual—and, when appropriate, homosexual—element in many if not all serious human relationships; but to stop there, to look no further to account for disappointment, feelings of betrayal, affection, need is to engage in severe reductionism.[4]

Psychoanalysis, as a form of interpretation, can show people that their symptoms are a veiled expression of discontent; and by so doing, can encourage them to make the necessary changes in their patterns of interacting so that the symptoms are not necessary (both because the patient can learn to express legitimate dissatisfaction directly, and because through understanding the distress itself can be cleared up). Ideally, then, psychoanalysis should be a force for radical social and sexual re-evaluation, allowing people to see the inappropriateness of ingrained social expectations and acquire the courage to cast them off. But this can be so only if the interpreter sees the distress that the symptoms represent as legitimate. If (as Freud did with Dora) a therapist recognizes that the symptoms signal unhappiness, but argues to his patient that her unhappiness is the result of her abnormality and perversity, the interpretations will have precisely the wrong effect: Rather than opening up new understanding and new possibilities, the power imbalance that interpretation assumes and reinforces will underline to the patient that the doctor is always right, she is the sick one, and she had better learn to put up with things as they are, terrible as they may be. This appears to be precisely the attitude with which (by Deutsch's testimony) Dora spent the rest of her discontented life.

Proponents of psychoanalysis correctly see the possibilities the interpretive method offers for deeper understanding and consequent liberation; but fail to appreciate the potential for abuse and the very great peril of misuse. They also fail to appreciate the fact that Freudian theories of psychosexual development, while technically independent of therapeutic method, condition the forms interpretations will take, as well as the rigidity with which their correctness is apt to be insisted on—especially, but by no means exclusively, by a male analyst dealing with a female patient.[5] An interpretation does not arise in the therapist's (or anyone's) mind out of nowhere, but is based on assumptions about what a cohesive and intelligible narrative is; how the world works; what is apt to be indirectly communicated; what people need and want, and should need and want. Such unexamined beliefs about sexual roles and behavior encourage interpretations of various sorts; and conservative ones will of course be reflected in interpretations that stress the "abnormality" of an unconventional mind. And an implicit presupposition (unlike the assertion itself, the interpretation) is not accessible to questioning or dispute by the patient, but nonetheless is present, coloring everything that is said.

The above discussion broaches another psychoanalytic unexamined concept, "normality." Recourse to such loaded, but unanalyzed, terms is dangerous. Freud takes exception to Dora's disgust at Herr K's embrace as "abnormal" and "neurotic." The very fact that we, coming upon the narrative a century later, see it quite differently shows that Freud is using the concept of "normality" in an idiosyncratic way. The problem is that the word has two distinct senses:

1. An action or attitude is "normal" if it is statistically more prevalent than other possibilities, that is, if it is what is usually encountered: "Normality" is roughly equivalent to predictability. This "normality" is demonstrable by surveys and direct observation; it is empirically falsifiable.
2. An action or attitude is "normal" if it is consonant with social, biological, or physiological utility: "Normality" is equated with appropriateness in some context. In this kind of definition, homosexuality, for example, would not be considered "normal" even if the majority of the population engaged in it, because it was not biologically useful, that is, directed toward reproduction. This is a much more dangerous use of the term (albeit probably the commonest popular use), since it makes use of pre-existing prejudices about what nature needs, or intends, which usually are not empirically observable. This is not the realm of science, but of ethics, or religion, or aesthetics.

Each of these uses has its valid sphere of reference. The danger arises when someone, speaking as a scientist, conflates the two definitions, in effect deriving a "scientific" justification of nonempirically validable claims from the fact that popular thinking validates (nonscientifically) the other. Freud, in *Dora* and elsewhere, regularly plays that game. The argument goes as follows:

A. A "normal" woman makes herself sexually available to a man (because most women are thought to do so, or at least are thought to be supposed to do so—another move away from demonstrability). This is "normality 2."
B. Normality 2 = Normality 1 (because the same word covers both).
C. Therefore, it is "scientifically" (that is, in terms of "normality 1") proved that Dora is neurotic (a "scientific" description; by "normality 2," she would be called wicked, or perverse). So the doctor has the right, and the obligation, to "cure" her. If the patient doesn't appreciate her "abnormality," that is merely another symptom of it, and only the doctor can make the diagnosis.

There is another way in which psychoanalytic thinking has been a damper on exploration rather than a force for change. In prescientific times, theological arguments tended to keep people in their place. One's role was defined by the Bible and the Church, and transgressors could expect punishment now or later. The Bible, and the Church, determined what was appropriate. During the nineteenth century, science began to supplant religion as the means by which to determine correct behavior or to enforce the status quo. Science became the judge of what was correct (again, with the conflation of the concepts of "correct" and "right" to include both moral and intellectual propriety). Now experts could invoke correct scientific understanding of the universe to account for the behavior of atoms, chromosomes, herring gulls, and, finally, people. Psychoanalysis had great influence on the last: It promised, as a science, to reduce human behavior to certain predictive laws, as physics and chemistry had done for the physical world. The problem was that the means of discovery, observation, and verification were by no means equivalent—a fact not given enough attention within the theory, and too often pooh-poohed when it was brought up.

So psychoanalysis proclaimed many of its discoveries and

laws as "scientific," meaning to equate them with the certainties of the physical sciences (hence the workings of the psyche were likened by Freud to the laws of fluid mechanics, and by more recent analytic theorists to the operations of computers), but lacking replicable experimental proof. And since the same words covered both territories, it was easy to beguile the reader into thinking that the arguments were truly "scientific." And just as previously an argument that cited Biblical authority was irrefutable, so now an argument based on "science" could not be disputed without the suspicion that one was acting under questionable motives. So conveniently enough, just as the legitimation of sexism by Biblical authority weakened its hold, "science" provided another validation. Psychoanalysis "scientized" sexism and thus made it respectable for the modern world; in the eyes of many, made it irrefutably right (cf. Eissler, 1977).

So the power imbalance between the sexes is strengthened by psychoanalysis in three ways: first, because its use of interpretation in therapy, most often by men upon women, utilizes the already existing stereotypes of sex roles and reinforces them; second, because it conflates two distinct senses of "normality" to suggest "scientifically" that a woman's traditional role is her only proper one; and finally, because it provides a "scientific" proof of male superiority.

Freud's discourse with Dora is more evidence of a tendency to use scientific method as a judgmental and punitive device to induce a young woman to accept her stereotypical role. It is not only *about* sexuality, it partakes of it in a rather disturbing way. Freud makes an extensive disavowal (pp. 48ff.) of any prurient motives in introducing to a virginal young girl sexual topics that, at that time, only the married, or perhaps only doctors, were supposed to know about. His defense is threefold: one, he is doing it in the interest of science; two, when a doctor talks about such things to a patient, prurience cannot enter into it; three, Dora knew about these things already. This defense is reminiscent of one Freud himself cites, in *Jokes and Their Relation to the Unconscious*—the rejoinder made by someone accused of returning a borrowed kettle in a damaged state: first, he never borrowed it; second, it had a hole in it already when he got it; third, he returned it undamaged. In any event, Freud has taught us that talking about sex often serves as a substitute for action, and that sexual innuendo between a man and a woman is often a symbolic equivalent of intercourse. In some ways, a therapist's insistence on initiating sexual topics with a woman who cannot see him, and whom he only imperfectly observes, is analogous to that of an anonymous obscene phone caller. It is different, of course, if the patient herself initiates the discourse, but here it is virtually always Freud who is the (verbal) aggressor. Freud's repeated intrusion of sexual matter into the conversation may well have been construed by Dora—who had already experienced unwanted sexual overtures from a man—as additional unwanted advances. And referring to acts and organs by euphemistic circumlocution, as Freud habitually does here as elsewhere, hardly exempts him from the charge of prurience. In medical practice, doctors do (to borrow Freud's adage) "appeller un chat un chat." But Freud doesn't: He calls it a pussy, and thereby exchanges the starched whites of the operating room for the silk and lace of the boudoir. Roundabout ways of talking about the forbidden, like clothing that appears to conceal but draws attention to what is being concealed, are erotically far more provocative than the straightforward words themselves, or technical medical terminology, or outright nudity. Freud's habit of hinting and guessing, rather than protecting the delicate sensibilities of a child, is more likely to arouse the very prurient curiosity that he so passionately disclaims—in the hearer to be sure, but in the speaker as well. (Recalling that much of Freud's argument in *Dora* rests on his claim that when a patient says no, she means yes, what are we to make of Freud's self-initiated, repeated, lengthy, and passionate denials of prurience?)

There is something else about the male therapist using language and raising ideas he knows will startle, if not shock. To be able to surprise someone in conversation is to assume, or reimpose, power both over the content of the discourse and over the hearer. To allow intrusion to pass unimpeded (as Dora does with Freud, though not with Herr K) is to implicitly acknowledge the dominance of the intruder. To show surprise, or shock, at someone else's conversational gambit is to acknowledge tacitly the other's victory, as well as the veiled threat behind what he is saying. So Freud's continually returning the dialogue to sexual matters is one more way he asserts and keeps control—regardless of whether he has "prurient" intent, whether it is normal medical practice, or whether Dora has heard it all already.[6]

There are several curious omissions in Freud's account, hard to explain if he is as perspicacious in discerning human motives as he is generally thought to be. On several occasions he accuses Dora of manipulativeness—over him, her father, and Herr K (manipulativeness is a charge he often levels at women). But if Dora is so manipulative, why doesn't she make more of an effort to manipulate Freud—that is, resort to the stereotypical feminine tactics that are supposed to win men over? If she senses (as surely she must) that Freud is not pleased with her clarity and assertiveness, why doesn't she change tactics and flirt, flatter, and ask for help? Freud can't have it both ways—that she is both manipulative and unfeminine.

In *Dora*, there are two especially problematic relationships: that of Dora and her mother, and that of Dora and Frau K. We learn early on that both Dora and her father have contempt for her mother. Here is surely pertinent information, if we wish to understand the distress of an adolescent girl. Since her one most natural role model is denied her, the possibility of a comfortable identification with the feminine role is made impossible. Most contemporary therapists, hearing such a report from a patient, would consider the situation pathogenic and devote much time to its exploration. (Certainly with the "Rat Man" and the "Wolf Man," a great deal of time is devoted to the [male] patient's hostility to his father.) But Freud takes the reports of the mother's inconsequence and ineptitude as true and unremarkable, and the issue is not examined at all. (Freud doesn't even note the probable causal relationship between the mother's syphilis and her compulsive housecleaning.) That Freud never examines in detail either Dora's or her father's statements (where Dora and her father agree, Freud does not question her); that he shows so little sympathy for the mother's condition; that he never wonders what effect it might have on an adolescent girl to despise her mother so totally, and be supported in this by her father—indicates, in someone usually so astute as Freud, a blindness most readily attributable to countertransference, and to his own identification, amply attested to in *Dora*, with Dora's father. Further, it seems to us, looking at the case in the light of current theory about the importance for adolescents of role models in identity formation, that a very serious difficulty Dora must have had, contributing in no small measure to her symptoms, was her contempt for the most important woman in her life.

If we accept the fact that Dora's negative perception of her mother made the latter impossible as a role model, her dependence on Frau K becomes readily intelligible, and her bitterness at Frau K's betrayal later, easy to understand. Both are the normal, and adaptive, responses of an adolescent girl looking for a model

of adult character and behavior on which to base her own matura-
tion. Her disappointment at Frau K's failure to fill that role would
be painful in any case, but all the more so if Dora had already been
disappointed once in her search, by her own mother. Whatever
"homosexual" threads there are in the fabric of Dora's attach-
ment to Frau K, the predominant motive seems to be the ego-
related one of identification. Freud's failure to recognize these
aspects of Dora's psyche certainly contributed to her despair. Additionally, here as elsewhere, he uses the imputation of homosexuality as a charge against Dora, like masturbation. (In both of these
areas, Freud has been hailed as a liberator, because he denied
that they were sinful or evil. It is less often recognized that he
nevertheless considered them as forms of sickness—neurosis or
perversion: another instance of the scientization of stigma.) These
charges are means of shaming Dora into submission, weapons he
holds over her head as forms of emotional—and for all we know,
given Freud's relationship with Dora's father, plausibly translated
into literal—blackmail. Finally, Freud uses his female patients'
"homosexuality" to rationalize their failure to develop a positive
erotic transference to him.

There is another interesting aspect to the representation of
the mother in the case history. The character Freud attributed to
her on the evidence of Dora herself and her father may not be
fully accurate. Freud, following his informants, characterizes the
mother as ineffectual and foolish. But if we look more closely at
her role vis-à-vis the others, another picture begins to emerge. The
roles possible for women—particularly if they were middle-aged,
untrained, and poorly educated—were severely circumscribed at
the turn of the century. Divorce, an easy option today, was then
more difficult legally and entailed a loss of social status and crea-
ture comforts that none but the inordinately courageous, or su-
premely desperate, would willingly risk. So for a woman in Dora's
mother's position, the intelligent choice was, somehow, to hang
onto the marriage, to present a favorable, or at least bearable,
picture of it to herself and the outside world. If her husband was
having affairs, it was the part of wisdom to act to the world as if
this were not the case: to indicate that the situation was not a
problem, so that she did not have to lose face by showing herself
as a woman who had lost her man, or be pushed by external
pressures into the social limbo entailed by divorce. A very strong
or powerful woman, ready to risk a great deal, might confront
her husband and demand that he break off the affair; but we have

seen what happened to Dora when she made that demand of her father, so we can assume that that was not apt to succeed for the mother (perhaps, for all we know, she had tried that route and failed).

So (supposing she could neither stop the affair nor separate) she was left with two possibilities: to complain fruitlessly to everyone, to acknowledge that Dora and the governess were correct in their perceptions, to make it clear that the marriage was a sham—and risk pity and contempt, with very little to gain; or she could be "stupid" and not see what was going on, and, if confronted, deny it with the same stolid determination. This is, of course, what she did—to her daughter's disgust. But she was acting in her own best interests and perhaps Dora's as well. There was much Dora did not yet know about real married life. The mother's choice was both the more difficult and the more intelligent. It called for great personal resources: the ability to keep quiet when confronted with painful information; the ability to go on living with, and caring for, a man she despised; the willingness to look stupid, to know she was being seen as contemptible, and yet persevere. Dora seems to the reader a young woman of considerable intellectual and moral strength. Perhaps, *pace* Freud, it was not her father from whom she inherited these gifts.

Another omission on Freud's part concerns the character of Herr K himself. There are many aspects of Herr K's character, as revealed in the narrative, that make him much less the "prepossessing" and thoroughly desirable mate a normal Dora should have wanted for life than Freud suggests to her, and the reader. For one thing, he appears to have had a taste for women who were extremely young. He was giving Dora presents and finding ways to spend unusual amounts of time with her from the time she was ten or so (and in current discussion of child sexual abuse, parents are always warned to be alert to just these signs). Frau K is several times described as "young," and so must be many years younger than her husband, who is in his forties, and has two children old enough to go about unchaperoned, so that she cannot have been out of adolescence when Herr K courted her; the Ks' governess, whom Herr K propositioned, is likewise described as a "young girl." What is significant here are Freud's lapses in interpretive skill, when Freud is precisely on target with every interpretation that reflects poorly on Dora's motives. This exemplifies the pragmatic use of interpretation as an aggressive weapon, rather than an educational tool. And Freud's notion that marriage—for Dora, and in general—ensured a woman's living a fairy-tale happily-ever-after life, suggests a childlike credulity startlingly at variance with the skeptical Freud who is presented to us elsewhere in his writings.

Freud's betrayal must have proved to Dora that she could not trust adults, especially men: hadn't their perfidy been demonstrated often enough? Erikson (1962) and Blos (1972) discuss (with Dora in mind) the dangers to an adolescent of being unable to find a trustworthy adult figure with whom to identify, or whom to use as a role model. She learns, further, to expect neither solicitude nor understanding—she is the culprit, not the victim, in adult eyes. Finally, Freud goes beyond the others in what may be the most damaging lesson of all. He teaches Dora to feel guilty for acts or thoughts that might allow her (with some guidance) to separate herself from her noxious family situation and cease to play the part assigned to her. Freud seals off that possibility; her dissatisfaction, he says, is dishonorable, due either to a desire for revenge based on (neurotic) unrequited love, or to (neurotic) needs based on prior guilty acts and thoughts (bed-wetting, thumb-sucking, masturbation, and homosexuality). So Dora's future unhappiness was effectively guaranteed by Freud's analysis, fragmentary though it was.

In his "postscript" to the case history, Freud argues that he failed because he was not sufficiently aware of the transference and was unable to interpret Dora's behavior to her in its terms. Freud says he realized belatedly that much of what Dora told him about the important men in her life could be understood as referring to Freud himself and to Dora's sexual feelings toward him. Because Freud failed to make these thoughts explicit to Dora, they were allowed to grow in importance in her mind, and since her feelings were unrequited, they developed into anger and a desire for revenge—satisfied, still according to Freud, by subverting the analysis. An additional cause for the unsatisfactory outcome, he suggests, perhaps a bit contradictorily, is his failure to realize the importance of, and interpret to Dora, her latent homosexuality, to make it clear that the role of the adult woman in Dora's life is best viewed not as friend, mentor, and role model, but as sex object—purely unconsciously, of course. We argue that the failure—if such it was (see below)—rests less on unresolved intrapsychic conflicts than on the interpersonal friction between analyst and analysand, based partly on the latter's series of prior betrayals, but more on the former's willful refusal to understand his patient—as a woman, and as a human being.

"If such it was"? Conventional wisdom (including our own commentary throughout this book) has always held that Dora's analysis ended in failure by not "bringing Dora to reason" in Freud's terms or, as we might put it today, bringing Dora to a state of healthy functioning, good self-esteem, and autonomy. But a cynic might argue that, looked at accurately, Freud *did* succeed with Dora, only too well. He "brought her to reason"—as "reason" was defined for a woman in Dora's time and place. He turned her into a woman such as Freud liked women to be: dependent, symptomatic, lacking in ambition, feeling helpless and incompetent. And by publishing the case history as a scientific demonstration, along with his other work, Freud as authority figure warns us all: Play the game. Don't violate the rules. Don't question authority. So the case history represents a success, for Freud and his world view. Freud "fixed" Dora, and with her, women everywhere.

Was the analysis a "success" or a "failure"? We cannot say. Perhaps the fact that this question cannot be answered represents yet another intriguing ambiguity of the case.

## NOTES

1. See, for instance, Chesler (1972), Chodorow (1978), Gilligan (1982), Miller (1976), Millett (1970), Rohrbaugh (1979), and Schafer (1974).

2. The tendency has always been to assume that the choice was either to resolve these issues as men did, that is, rightly, or as women did, or badly; and to see the male way as "normal," the female as perverse. So the best women could do was to argue that, in fact, they *could* under optimal conditions achieve the moral stance of men. More recently Gilligan (1982) has argued for a wholly different position: Males and females do indeed have different moralities, the former being as Freud suggested generalizing and group-oriented, the latter tailored to individual needs and situations. But one is not intrinsically better, just different.

3. These arguments may seem somewhat archaic, a throwback to a less developed stage of psychoanalytic theory. But a glance at the most recent Chicago Psychoanalytic Index, the definitive bibliographical listing in the field, for 1987–88, shows some 10 listings under the heading of "penis envy," suggesting that the issue is still alive, at least alive enough to be controversial. Theorists like Schafer (1974) have presented courageous revi-

sions of Freud's theories of female sexuality; but lest it seem as though the battle is over, we should remember the very influential rejoinder of Galenson and Roiphe (1980), arguing that penis envy is a real entity: a position still perfectly acceptable within the orthodoxy. Their "empirical" reasoning: Little girls display interest in the genitalia of little boys. An outsider might argue that this observation is scarcely empirical proof of penis envy per se, let alone its theoretical concomitants, but merely evidence that small children, like the rest of us, are interested in other people's things.

4. If Dora's emotional closeness to Frau K constituted presumptive evidence of "homosexuality," what are we to make of Freud's frequently passionate declarations in his letters to Wilhelm Fliess?

5. It is sometimes suggested that women can avoid the abuses of male-centered therapy by choosing female therapists. While it is more probable that a woman will be free of male sexual stereotypes than will a man, vigilance is still necessary. Not every woman is a feminist; not every self-proclaimed "feminist" is a feminist. Especially in traditional psychoanalysis, which is still male-dominated numerically and theoretically, women often feel a need to adopt the values and stereotypes of their male colleagues to prove to the power hierarchy that they are worthy of admission to the club: They become "honorary men." So a woman like Helene Deutsch has, in her theoretical work (and undoubtedly in her practice), done as much harm to the female psyche as any of her more obviously sexist male colleagues.

6. Maddi (1974) sees Dora as victimized by Freud's linguistic "prurience," as well as her family's "web of corruption" and her society's relegation of women to secondary status. As he says,

And *his* [Freud's] form of sexual activity, practicing psychotherapy, corresponded nicely to the patient's having symptoms. This makes the "drugged" feeling Freud reported after Dora left therapy a hysterical symptom representing the satiety following orgasm. (p. 100)

# 9

# Summary and Conclusions

We have argued that Freud, in diagnosing and treating Dora's illness, was responding first to the needs of his society and himself as a member of that society; second to her father on whom she was dependent and whom he considered a friend (and who, not coincidentally, was paying the bills); and hardly at all to the needs of his patient, a desperate young woman for whom he was the last resort and whom, therefore, he failed. We see that the shrewdest therapist's perspicacity may desert him when it comes into conflict with his milieu and his society, and that, in this case—necessarily, in every such case—it is the patient who suffers. We see, further, that *Dora* raises once more the issue discussed by Szasz (1974) and others: the requirement that in undertaking individual treatment the therapist be acting unambiguously as the agent of the patient—not the patient's family, or society, or any other person or institution.

The patient needs also to be protected—as Dora was not— from the potential damage that may be done by a therapist misusing the otherwise essential therapeutic power imbalance. It may be true that a good therapist—and a relatively healthy patient— will not let things get out of hand; but what guarantee is there that this situation will always obtain? The psychotherapeutic establishment has for too long sanguinely assumed that all therapists could behave according to the standards for good therapy that Freud set forth in writing—and has been oblivious of his disregard for those standards in practice, by his own testimony. There are bylaws in medical and psychotherapeutic professional societies, and legislation mandating criminal penalties, discouraging the sexual or financial exploitation of patients by therapists, and this is as it should be. But there are none to discourage other, subtler forms of exploitation based on the power imbalance; indeed, there has been no way of talking about it, nor is it even considered abnormal or exploitative by most practitioners. But psychological exploitation via interpretation is but one end of the continuum of power asymmetry of which sexual exploitation is the other, and they are really the same phenomenon, and equally dangerous. Freud may never have dealt with any of his patients in a sexually exploitative way, but at least as much damage can be done at the other end of the continuum. It may well be impossible to prevent, as long as therapists (male and female alike) treat female clients without having examined the implications of being male and female in a society with the prejudices of ours.

We have tried, in the foregoing discussion, to relate the disaster of *Dora* less to some specific lack of skill or insight in Freud or to the malaise of Victorian society (which would imply that there was no longer such a risk) than to the inherent power imbalance in the therapeutic situation and its potential for abuse. The abuse was facilitated by Freud's own personality and social milieu superimposed upon the power imbalance between men and women, and the fact that this imbalance is obscured and rationalized by the culture in which it occurs, as well as by a therapeutic system that equates what is with what should and must be, in psychosexual dynamics. The use in psychoanalysis of unilateral interpretation both draws from and reasserts this imbalance.

It is probably futile to try to take precautions against repetitions of the *Dora* fiasco by establishing rules for the surface forms of therapeutic interaction; it is the situation itself that creates the danger, and this situation has not materially altered, and will not as long as the basic conditions present in *Dora* are still in effect. External changes can be, and frequently are, made, to give the appearance of a more egalitarian relationship between therapist and patient: mutual first-naming, eye contact, and expressions of patient autonomy. But since the basic power imbalance cannot be eradicated, it should at least be explicitly recognized by both participants in the therapeutic discourse—which would entail a total revision of therapeutic theory and technique—Freud's experience with Dora (and, worse, Dora's with Freud) is apt to be repeated, again and again, in the name of "cure."

While it is outside the scope of this book to make explicit prescriptions for change in psychotherapeutic technique, we can make a few general suggestions in the direction of a more egalitarian relationship, which would limit the potential for abuse. First and most crucially, the field must dispense with the cardinal rule that "the patient is always wrong," that a patient's objection to any aspect of the therapeutic environment is necessarily motivated by unconscious pathology, rather than by failings on the analyst's part, or a mismatch in the personalities of the participants, or a misunderstanding between them. In a therapeutic system one of whose principal aims is to help the patient achieve a greater degree of autonomy, it is imperative that the latter learn, from early on, that if anything seems confusing or wrong, intellectually or morally, it is intrinsic to the process that it be discussed and dealt with to the satisfaction of both participants. As the patient grows more skillful and courageous in participating in the process of therapy, he or she should be entrusted with ever greater responsibility for directing the process itself—interpretation, reconstruction, and the devising of operative metaphors.

This prescription may seem visionary, and will certainly seem, to the orthodox, violently antianalytic, certain to hinder the development of the transference and the regression necessary for the work of analysis. But the relation between improvement and regression has yet to be proved[1]; what is certainly proved is the relation between a patient's regression and potential for suffering the sort of abuse Dora underwent. If it is agreed that autonomy is a significant aspect of mental health and happiness in this culture, and that therefore it is to be encouraged as part of successful therapy, we must look askance at a mode of treatment that militates against it.

We suggest a revision in the ideal of treatment so as to emphasize a more fully egalitarian attitude, in which patient and therapist from the start both understand that each shares in the responsibility to make the discourse succeed. Success then is to be defined in terms of the patient or client's, rather than the therapist's, goals. As part of their training, therapists should be exposed to current thinking in a wide range of areas in the social sciences, emphasizing the current political structures of the society and their implications for therapeutic misunderstanding and abuse. They should also receive training in communication theories: cross-cultural sociolinguistics, for instance, which will point out ways in which two people from different cultures, genders, or social strata can, with the best will in the world, misunderstand each other; and pragmatics, which relates the forms of language to their functions and describes options and consequences of individual styles. The therapeutic relationship will never be fully egalitarian; but no professional relationships are: Professionals, after all, are consulted because they have skills that their clients do not. In the case of therapy, the application of those skills requires that the therapist have unilateral and nonreciprocal access to the client's internal and external communicative processes. But with new kinds of training for the therapist, and discussion between therapist and client before the beginning of therapy proper about their respective responsibilities and rights, and about the aims of therapy, it is to be hoped that the potential for abuse will be lessened, if not eliminated.

## NOTE

1. Indeed, an outcome study of clients (Wallerstein, 1986, 1989) treated at the Menninger Clinic found that patients receiving simple supportive treatment fared as well as those receiving psychoanalysis.

# References

Austin, J. L. (1962). *How to do things with words.* Oxford: Oxford University Press.

Bateson, Gregory. (1972). *Steps to an ecology of mind.* New York: Ballantine.

Becker, Howard S. (1964). *Outsiders: Studies in the sociology of deviance.* New York: Free Press.

Bernheimer, Charles, & Kahane, Claire (Eds.). (1985). *In Dora's case.* New York: Columbia University Press.

Bernstein, Basil. (1962). Linguistic codes, hesitation phenomena, and intelligence. *Language and Speech, 5,* 31–46.

Blos, Peter. (1972). The epigenesis of the adult neurosis. *Psychoanalytic Study of the Child, 27,* 106–134.

Breuer, Joseph, & Freud, Sigmund. (1956). Studies on hysteria: Anna O. *Standard edition* (Vol. II, pp. 21–47). (Original work published 1893–95)

Broverman, Inge K., Broverman, Donald M., Clarkson, Frank E., Rosenkrantz, Paul S., & Vogel, Susan R. (1970). Sex-role stereotypes and clinical judgments of mental health. *Journal of Consulting and Clinical Psychology, 34*(1), 1–7.

Brown, Penelope, & Levinson, Stephen. (1986). *Politeness: Some universals in language.* Cambridge: Cambridge University Press.

Chesler, Phyllis. (1972). *Women and madness.* New York: Avon.

Chodorow, Nancy. (1978). *The reproduction of mothering.* Berkeley: University of California Press.

Chomsky, Noam. (1965). *Aspects of the theory of syntax.* Cambridge, MA: MIT Press.

Collins, Jerre, Green, J. Ray, Lydon, Mary, Sachner, Mark, & Skoller, Eleanor H. (1983, Spring). Questioning the unconscious: The Dora archives. *Diacritics,* pp. 37–42. (Reprinted in Bernheimer & Kahane)

Coyne, James C. (1976). Toward an interactive description of depression. *Psychiatry, 39,* 28–40.

Coyne, James C. (1985). Toward a theory of frames and reframing: The social nature of frames. *Journal of Marital and Family Therapy, 11,* 337–344.

Coyne, James C. (1987). The concept of empowerment in strategic therapy. *Psychotherapy, 24*, 539–545.

Coyne, James C. (1988). Employing therapeutic paradox in the treatment of depression. In M. L. Ascher (Ed.), *Therapeutic paradox*. New York: Guilford Press.

Coyne, James C., & Widiger, Thomas. (1979). Toward a participatory model of psychotherapy. *Professional Psychology, 10*, 8–14.

Dahl, Hartwig, Teller, Virginia, Moss, Donald, & Trujillo, Manuel. (1978). Countertransference examples of the syntactic expression of warded-off contents. *Psychoanalytic Quarterly, 47*, 339–363.

Daly, Mary. (1978). *Gyn/Ecology*. Boston: Free Press.

Decker, Hannah. (1990). *Freud, Dora, and Vienna 1900*. New York: Free Press.

Deutsch, Felix. (1957). A footnote to Freud's "Fragment of an analysis of a case of hysteria." *Psychoanalytic Quarterly, 26*, 159–167. (Reprinted in Bernheimer & Kahane)

Edelson, Marshall. (1975). *Language and interpretation in psychoanalysis*. New Haven and London: Yale University Press.

Eissler, Kurt. (1977). Comments on penis envy and orgasm in women. *Psychoanalytic Study of the Child, 32*, 29–83.

Erickson, Bonnie, Lind, E. Allen, Johnson, Bruce C., & O'Barr, William M. (1978). Speech style and impression in a court setting: The effects of "powerful" and "powerless" language. *Journal of Experimental and Social Psychology, 14*, 266–279.

Erikson, Erik H. (1962). Reality and actuality. *Journal of the American Psychoanalytic Association, 10*, 451–474. (Reprinted in Bernheimer & Kahane)

Fillmore, Charles. (1971). Verbs of judging. In C. Fillmore & D. T. Langendoen (Eds.), *Studies in linguistic semantics*. New York: Holt, Rinehart and Winston.

Freud, Sigmund. (1953). The interpretation of dreams. In J. Strachey (Ed. and trans.). *The standard edition of the complete psychological works of Sigmund Freud*. London: The Hogarth Press and the Institute of Psychoanalysis. (Vols. IV–V). (Original work published 1900)

Freud, Sigmund. (1953). Fragment of an analysis of a case of hysteria. *Standard edition* (Vol. VII, pp. 3–122). (Original work published 1905)

Freud, Sigmund. (1955). Notes upon a case of obsessional neurosis. *Standard edition* (Vol. X, pp. 153–320). (Original work published 1909)

Freud, Sigmund. (1955). From the history of an infantile neurosis. *Standard edition* (Vol. XVII, pp. 3–122). (Original work published 1918)

Freud, Sigmund. (1955). The psychogenesis of a case of female homosexuality. *Standard edition* (Vol. XVIII, pp. 145–172). (Original work published 1920)

Freud, Sigmund. (1957). The antithetical meaning of primal words. *Standard edition* (Vol. XI, pp. 155–161). (Original work published 1910)

Freud, Sigmund. (1958). Papers on technique: On beginning the treatment (further recommendations on the technique of psycho-analysis I). *Standard edition* (Vol. XII, pp. 121–144). (Original work published 1913)

Freud, Sigmund. (1959). The question of lay analysis. *Standard edition* (Vol. XX, pp. 183–258). (Original work published 1926)

Freud, Sigmund. (1961). The ego and the id. *Standard edition* (Vol. XIX, pp. 12–66). (Original work published 1923)

Freud, Sigmund. (1961). The dissolution of the Oedipus complex. *Standard edition* (Vol. XIX, pp. 173–179). (Original work published 1924)

Freud, Sigmund. (1961). Some psychical consequences of the anatomical differences between the sexes. *Standard edition* (Vol. XIX, pp. 248–258). (Original work published 1925)

Freud, Sigmund. (1961). Female sexuality. *Standard edition* (Vol. XXI, pp. 225–243). (Original work published 1931)

Freud, Sigmund. (1963). Introductory lectures on psycho-analysis, part III, lecture XXVIII. Analytic therapy. *Standard edition* (Vol. XVI, pp. 448–463). (Original work published 1916–17)

Galenson, Eleanor, & Roiphe, Herman. (1980). Some suggested revisions concerning early female sexual development. In M. Kirkpatrick (Ed.), *Women's sexual development* (pp. 83–105). New York: Plenum Press.

Gallop, Jane. (1982). Keys to Dora. In J. Gallop (Ed.), *The daughter's seduction: Feminism and psychoanalysis* (Chapter 9). Ithaca, NY: Cornell University Press. (Reprinted in Bernheimer & Kahane)

Gearhart, Suzanne. (1979, Spring). The scene of psychoanalysis: The unanswered questions of Dora. *Diacritics*, pp. 11–126. (Reprinted in Bernheimer & Kahane)

Gilligan, Carol. (1982). *In a different voice.* Cambridge, MA: Harvard University Press.

Glaser, Barney G., & Strauss, Anselm L. (1964). Awareness contexts and social interactions. *American Sociological Review, 29,* 669–679.

Glenn, Jules. (1978). Freud's adolescent patients: Katherina, Dora, and "the homosexual woman." In M. Kanzer & J. Glenn (Eds.), *Freud and his patients.* New York: Jason Aronson.

Goleman, Daniel. (1990, March 6). As a therapist, Freud fell short, scholars find. *The New York Times*, pp. B5, B9.

Greenson, Ralph. (1967). *The technique and practice of psychoanalysis.* New York: International Universities Press.

Grice, H. P. (1975). Logic and conversation. In P. Cole & J. Morgan (Eds.), *Syntax and semantics: Vol. III. Speech acts* (pp. 41–58). New York: Academic Press.

Grünbaum, Adolf. (1984). *The foundations of psychoanalysis: A philosophical critique.* Berkeley: The University of California Press.

Gumperz, John. (1982). *Social identity.* Cambridge: Cambridge University Press.

Habermas, Jurgen. (1971). *Knowledge and human interests* (J. J. Shapiro, Trans.). Boston: Beacon Press.

Haley, Jay. (1973). *Uncommon psychotherapy: The psychiatric techniques of Milton H. Erickson*. New York: Moulton.

Halliday, M. A. K., & Hasan, Ruqaiya. (1976). *Cohesion in English*. London: Longman.

Hare-Mustin, Rachel. (1983). An appraisal of the relationship between women and psychotherapy: Eighty years after the case of Dora. *American Psychologist, 38*, 593–601.

Heilbrun, Carolyn. (1990). *Hamlet's mother and other women*. New York: Ballantine.

Hertz, Neil. (1983, Spring). Dora's secrets, Freud's techniques. *Diacritics*, pp. 65–76. (Reprinted in Bernheimer & Kahane)

Jennings, Jerry L. (1986). The revival of "Dora." *Journal of the American Psychoanalytic Association, 34*(3), 607–635.

Labov, William, & Fanshel, David. (1977). *Therapeutic discourse: Psychotherapy as conversation*. New York: Academic Press.

Lacan, Jacques. (1966). *Ecrits* (Alan Sheridan-Smith, Trans.). New York: Norton.

Laing, R. D. (1967). *The politics of experience*. London: Penguin.

Lakoff, Robin Tolmach. (1978a). Review of M. Edelson, *Language and interpretation in psychoanalysis*. *Language*, pp. 377–394.

Lakoff, Robin Tolmach. (1978b). Stylistic strategies in a grammar of style. In J. Orasanu, M. K. Slater, and L. L. Adler (Eds.), *Language, Sex, and Gender*. Annals of The New York Academy of Science, vol. 327, pp. 53–78.

Lakoff, Robin Tolmach. (1982). The rationale of psychotherapeutic discourse. In J. Anchin & D. Kiesler (Eds.), *Handbook of interpersonal psychotherapy* (pp. 132–146). New York: Pergamon.

Lakoff, Robin Tolmach. (1990). *Talking power: The politics of language in daily life*. New York: Basic Books.

Langs, Robert. (1976). The misalliance dimension in Freud's case histories. *International Journal of Psychoanalytic Psychotherapy, 5*, 301–318.

Lewin, Kurt. (1974). Dora revisited. *Psychoanalytic Review, 60*, 519–532.

Lichtman, Richard. (1982). *The production of desire: The integration of psychoanalysis and Marxist theory*. New York: Free Press.

Loftus, Elizabeth. (1979). *Eyewitness testimony*. Cambridge, MA: Harvard University Press.

Luborsky, Lester, Singer, Barton, & Luborsky, Lise. (1975). Comparative studies of psychotherapies: Is it true that "everyone must win and all must have prizes"? *Archives of General Psychiatry, 32*(8), 995–1008.

Maddi, Salvatore. (1974, September). The victimization of Dora. *Psychology Today*, pp. 91–100.

Malcolm, Janet. (1984, December 20). Review of M. M. Gill, *Analysis of transference: Vol. I: Theory and technique*; M. M. Gill & I. Z. Hoffman, *Vol. II: Studies of nine audio-recorded psychoanalytic sessions*. *New York Review of Books*, pp. 13ff.

Marcus, Steven. (1975). Freud and Dora: Story, history, case-history. In *Representations*. New York: Random House. (Reprinted in Bernheimer & Kahane)

Masson, Jeffrey Moussaieff. (1983). *The assault on truth*. New York: Farrar, Straus, and Giroux.

Masson, Jeffrey Moussaieff. (1988). *Against therapy*. New York: Atheneum.

McCaffrey, Phillip. (1984). *Freud and Dora: The artful dream*. New Brunswick, NJ: Rutgers University Press.

Miller, Jean Baker. (1976). *Toward a new psychoanalysis of women*. New York: Beacon Press.

Millett, Kate. (1970). *Sexual politics*. New York: Doubleday.

Mitchell, Juliet. (1974). *Psychoanalysis and feminism*. New York: Pantheon.

Moi, Toril. (1981). Representation of patriarchy: Sexuality and epistemology in Freud's Dora. *Feminist Review, 9*, 60–73. (Reprinted in Bernheimer & Kahane)

Muslin, Hyman, & Gill, Merton. (1978). Transference in the Dora case. *Journal of the American Psychoanalytic Association, 26*, 311–328.

Omer, Haim, & Alon, Nahman. (1989). Principles of psychotherapeutic strategy. *Psychotherapy, 26*, 282–289.

Pletsch, Carl. (1982). Freud's case studies. *Partisan Review, 49*, 101–118.

Popper, Karl R. (1962). *Conjectures and refutations: The growth of scientific knowledge*. New York: Basic Books.

Ramas, Maria. (1980). Freud's Dora, Dora's hysteria: The negation of a woman's rebellion. *Feminist Studies, 6*(3), 472–510. (Reprinted in Bernheimer & Kahane)

Ricoeur, Paul. (1981). *Hermeneutics and the human sciences* (J. B. Thompson, Trans.). Cambridge: Cambridge University Press.

Rieff, Philip. (1963). Introduction. In *Dora, an analysis of a case of hysteria* (Joan Riviere, Trans.). New York: Collier.

Rohrbaugh, Joanna B. (1979). *Women: Psychology's puzzle*. New York: Basic Books.

Schafer, Roy. (1974). Problems in Freud's psychology of women. *Journal of the American Psychoanalytic Association, 22*, 459–485.

Schafer, Roy. (1976). *A new language for psychoanalysis*. New Haven: Yale University Press.

Schafer, Roy. (1980, Autumn). Narration in the psychoanalytic dialogue. *Critical Inquiry*, pp. 29–53.

Schafer, Roy. (1983). *The analytic attitude*. New York: Basic Books.

Schofield, William. (1964). *Psychotherapy: The purchase of friendship*. Englewood Cliffs, NJ: Prentice-Hall.

Shapiro, David. (1965). *Neurotic styles*. New York: Basic Books.

Singer, Margaret T., Wynne, Lyman C., & Tookey, Margaret L. (1978). Communication disorders and the families of schizophrenics. In L. C. Wynne, R. L. Cromwell, & S. Mattysse (Eds.), *The nature of schizophrenia*. New York: Wiley.

Sluzki, Carlos. (1981). Process of symptom formation and patterns of symptom maintenance. *Journal of Marital and Family Therapy, 7,* 273–280.

Spence, Donald. (1982). *Narrative truth and historical truth.* New York: Norton.

Spence, Donald. (1986). When interpretation masquerades as explanation. *Journal of the American Psychoanalytic Association, 34*(1), 3–21.

Sprengnether, Madelon. (1985). Enforcing Oedipus: Freud and Dora. In Charles Bernheimer & Claire Kahane (Eds.), *In Dora's case* (pp. 254–275). New York: Columbia University Press.

Stierlin, Helm. (1976). The dynamics of owning and disowning. *Family Process, 15*(3), 277–288.

Strachey, James. (1934). The nature of the therapeutic action of psychoanalysis. *International Journal of Psychoanalysis, 15,* 127–159.

Szasz, Thomas. (1974). *The ethics of psychoanalysis.* New York: Basic Books (Colophon).

Tannen, Deborah. (1990). *You just don't understand.* New York: William Morrow.

Van Dijk, Teun A. (Ed.). (1976). *Pragmatics of language and literature.* Amsterdam: North Holland.

Waelder, Robert. (1936). The principle of multiple function. *Psychoanalytic Quarterly,* pp. 45–62.

Wallerstein, Robert S. (1986). *Forty-two lives in treatment: A study of psychoanalysis and psychotherapy. The report of the Menninger Foundation, 1954–1982.* New York: Guilford Press.

Wallerstein, Robert S. (1989). The psychotherapy project of the Menninger Foundation. *Journal of Consulting and Clinical Psychology, 57,* 195–203.

Watzlawick, Paul, Beavin, Janet, & Jackson, Don D. (1967). *Pragmatics of human communication.* New York: Norton.

Watzlawick, Paul, Weakland, John, & Fisch, Richard. (1974). *Change: Principles of problem formation and problem resolution.* New York: Norton.

Yalom, Irvin D. (1989). *Love's executioner.* New York: HarperCollins.

Zetzel, E. (1956). Current concepts of transference. *International Journal of Psychoanalysis, 37,* 369–376.

# Index

Abusive relationship, 2–4, 6–7, 8–10, 13, 132–135
Adjustment, 116–117
Adolescence, 29, 30, 100, 126
Adversarial model, 81–82, 84, 89
Alon, Nahman, 67
Ambiguity, 48, 50, 55, 65, 69
Analytic theory/theorists, 10–11, 113
Anamnesis, 3, 62, 91
Anger, of Dora, 20, 120, 121, 129
"Anna O.," 86, 88–89, 105
Antitherapy movement, 14
*Armies of the Night* (Mailer), 32
Art, and science, 33, 34, 45
Austin, J. L., 55–56
Awareness context, 100–101

Bateson, Gregory, 24–25, 58n1
Bauer, Ida. *See* Dora (person)
Beavin, Janet, 5, 59n3
Becker, Howard S., 74–75, 109
Bernheimer, Charles, 1, 35, 14n1, 76n5
Bernstein, Basil, 93
Blos, Peter, 29, 30, 129
Breuer, Joseph, 86, 88–89
Brief therapy, 25, 66
"Bringing client to reason," 20, 38–39, 74, 91, 130
Broverman, Inge K., 117
Brown, Penelope, 57

Capote, Truman, 32
"Case of Female Homosexuality" (Freud), 86, 87, 115
Case history
    and concentric circles of text, 78
    as an exemplary case, 33

as a history of miscommunication, 78
as a literary narrative, 31–34, 78
purpose of, 23
as a scientific document, 31, 32, 33, 34, 78
as textual genre, 92–93
and truth, 33
Change
    in analytic theory, 10–11
    and communication, 43, 70–71
    of language habits, 61, 62, 63, 70–71, 115–117, 120
    and myth, 67
    and psychotherapy, 5, 116–117, 121
Chesler, Phyllis, 3, 35, 130n1
Chicago Psychoanalytic Index, 130n3
Chodorow, Nancy, 112, 130n1
Chomsky, Noam, 34, 45, 72
Class issues, and power, 24
Collaboration, between therapist and client, 90–91, 133–135
Collins, Jerre, 35, 37
Communication. *See also* Direct discourse; Discourse; Therapeutic discourse
    as basis of psychological problems, 43–44, 66, 67–68
    as basis of therapy, 26
    and change, 43, 70–71
    and egalitarianism, 134–135
    and group therapy, 24–25
    importance of, 40–41
    intent of, 117
    and interpretation, 63
    and the Lacanians, 24
    need for therapist training in, 134
    and pragmatics, 40
    as text/discourse, 89

Confrontation, 66, 119
Conversational logic, 50–54, 56
Cooperative principle, 51–54, 71, 118
Couple therapy, 25, 77–78
Coyne, James C., 5, 100, 106
Cultural psychoanalysis, 24, 28–29, 133

Dahl, Hartwig, 59n2
Daly, Mary, 35
Decker, Hannah, 1, 10, 38, 39
Deutsch, Felix, 20–21, 77, 88, 121, 76n5, 97n2
Deutsch, Helene, 39, 131n5
Development stages, 103–104
Direct discourse, 82–84, 87
Discourse. See also Direct discourse; Therapeutic discourse
    communication as, 89
    forms of, 76n6
    private/public, 93–94
"Door-a," 36–37
Dora (case history)
    as "Door-a," 36–37
    as a failure for Freud, 5–6, 129–130, 132
    as a fragment of an analysis, 1, 79
    Freud's interpersonal problems in, 80–96, 129–130
    Freud's omissions in, 125–129
    as a generalized situation, 13–14
    importance of, 24
    as a literary text, 80, 93–95
    reasons for interest in, 1–4
    as a scientific text, 78, 79–80, 93–95, 130
    summary of, 15–20
    and the "text" of analysis, 91
    as a training manual, 3
    as a trial, 81, 84, 90
Dora (person)
    anger of, 20, 120, 121, 129
    and blame for the situation, 129
    development stages of, 103–104
    "fantasies" of, 19, 74, 104–105
    father as instigator of, seeking treatment, 100, 109–110
    Freud's role in future happiness/unhappiness of, 20–21, 129, 97n2
    as a heroine, 76n5

possible outcomes for, 108–109
source of problems of, 4–5
as a victim, 39, 76n5, 131n6
Dreams, 28, 66

Edelson, Marshall, 34
Egalitarianism in psychoanalysis, 71–72, 133–134, 75–76n4
Ego psychology, 23, 24
Eissler, Kurt, 7, 124
Erickson, Bonnie, 116
Erikson, Erik, 3, 30, 88–89, 90, 108, 129
Ethics of therapy, 75, 132–133
Explanation, 34, 56, 93

"Face" concept, 57–58
"Factions," 32
Factuality, 94–96
Family situation, of Dora, 15–16, 29, 38, 100–110
Family therapy, 25, 77–78
Fanshel, David, 12
"Fantasies" of Dora, 19, 74, 104–105
Father of Dora
    and the case history summary, 15, 16, 17, 18, 19, 20, 21
    Freud's identification with, 91–92, 126, 127, 98n5
    as instigator of Dora's seeking treatment, 100, 109–110
    and the interpersonal framework, 100–110
    and possible outcomes for Dora, 108–109
Fathers, as major force affecting children, 112
Female therapists, 131n5
Feminine psychology. See also Gender issues
    Freud's views of, 87–88, 111–112, 115, 120–121, 130, 133, 130–131n3
    and interpretation, 122
    and sexual matters, 16–17, 18, 24, 73–74, 113–114, 119–120, 122, 124–125, 129
Feminists, 3–5, 7, 22–23, 25, 26, 35–38, 112, 76n5, 131n5
Fillmore, Charles, 63

Fisch, Richard, 5
Frau K
  and the case history summary, 17,
    18, 19
  Dora's relationship with, 126–127,
    131n4
  and the interpersonal framework,
    100–110
  and possible outcomes for Dora,
    108–109
Freud, Sigmund
  and an adversarial model, 81–82
  and analytic neutrality, 97n1
  case histories of, 86
  and feminine psychology/women,
    87–88, 111–112, 115, 120–121,
    130, 133, 130–131n3
  identification with Dora's father/
    Herr K of, 91–92, 126, 127,
    132, 98n5
  and linguistic theory, 44
  and meaningfulness in communica-
    tion, 65
  medical analogy of, 6–7
  and overdetermination, 59n3
  reconstruction/note-taking method
    of, 12–13
  and the scientific method, 124
  and the social environment, 109
  style of, 98n4
  and therapeutic discourse, 70

Galenson, Eleanor, 130–131n3
Gallop, Jane, 35, 36–37
Gearhart, Suzanne, 35
Gender issues
  and interpretation, 124
  and language, 115–116
  and neurotics, 65
  and power, 2–4, 8, 13, 113–115,
    124
  and science, 124
Gill, Merton, 26–27
Gilligan, Carol, 130n1, 130n2
Glaser, Barney G., 100
Glenn, Jules, 103
Goleman, Daniel, 76n5
Green, J. Ray, 35
Greenson, Ralph, 63
Grice, H. P., 51–54, 71

Group therapy, 24–25
Grunbaum, Adolf, 41n2, 75n3
Gumperz, John, 93

Habermas, Jurgen, 13, 72, 75n3
Haley, Jay, 105
Halliday, M. A. K., 63
Hamlet (Shakespeare), 32–33
Hare-Mustin, Rachel, 117
Hasan, Ruqaiya, 63
Heilbrun, Carolyn, 39
Hermeneutics, 13
Herr K
  and the case history summary, 16,
    17, 18–20, 21
  and cultural critics, 28
  Freud's identification with, 91, 98n5
  Freud's omissions about, 128–129
  and the interpersonal framework,
    101–110
  and possible outcomes for Dora,
    108–109
  and transference/countertransfer-
    ence, 27
Hertz, Neil, 35, 37, 89, 98n4
Homonymy, 48, 59n3
Homosexuality, 11, 27, 28, 114, 121,
    127, 129, 131n4
Horney, Karen, 24, 39
Hyperbole, 118, 119
Hysteria, 1, 5, 20, 21, 100, 105, 118,
    119, 120, 131n6

Implicature, 11, 52–53, 54, 55, 56, 118
Incest, 29–30
In Cold Blood (Capote), 32
Indirectness, 11, 53–54, 55, 56–57,
    58, 61, 65, 107, 117, 118–119
Inner dialogue, 61–62
Insight-oriented therapy, 72
Interpersonal problems, and the Freud-
    Dora relationship, 77–98, 129–130
Interpersonal systems theory, 4, 5, 25,
    31–40, 99–110
Interpretation. See also Interpersonal
    systems theory; Intrapsychic
    therapy
  benefits of method of, 121
  and case histories, 93
  and change, 121

Interpretation (*continued*)
and communication, 63
correcting, 71–72
corroboration of, 41–42*n*2
as definition, 63–64
*Dora* as an illustration and legitimation for methods of, 3
dream, 28
and explanation, 34
and feminine psychology, 122, 124
and Freud's omissions, 128–129
and literary texts, 25–26, 93
and power, 13, 64–66, 71–72, 73, 114, 115, 117–118, 121
and pragmatics, 64, 75*n*1
psychoanalysis as a form of, 121
questions about the nature of, 13
and reciprocity, 75–76*n*4
and semantics, 62–63, 64, 71, 75*n*1
and style, 49–50
and values, 11, 64
Intersubjectivity, 72–73
Intrapsychic therapy, 3, 4–5, 6, 10, 23–24, 29, 30, 31, 39, 72, 74
Irony, 58, 118, 119

Jackson, Don D., 5, 59*n*3
Jennings, Jerry L., 26
Johnson, Bruce C., 116
*Jokes and Their Relation to the Unconscious* (Freud), 124

Kahane, Claire, 1, 35–36, 14*n*1, 76*n*5
K family. *See* Frau K; Herr K

Labov, William, 12
Lacan, Jacques, 1, 4, 23–24
Lacanians, 22, 23–24
Laing, R. D., 25, 58*n*1
Lakoff, Robin Tolmach, 57, 116
Langs, Robert, 108
Language learning/changing language, 61, 62, 63, 70–71, 115–117, 120, 134–135
Levinson, Stephen, 57
Lewin, Kurt, 7, 27–28
Lichtman, Richard, 4, 38
Life stories, 89–90
Lind, E. Allen, 116

Linguistics/philosophy of language, 27–28, 34, 44–50, 51, 60, 62, 73
Literary/text critics, 4, 22–23, 25–26, 28–29, 31–33, 34
Literary texts
case histories as, 31–34, 78
characteristics of, 93–95
"Little Hans," 86
Loftus, Elizabeth, 12, 98*n*3
Logical positivists, 54, 55
Luborsky, Lester, 67
Luborsky, Lise, 67
Lydon, Mary, 35

McCaffrey, Phillip, 28
Maddi, Salvatore, 39, 131*n*5
Mailer, Norman, 32
Malcolm, Janet, 75–76*n*4
Manipulation, 72, 73–74, 125–126
Marcus, Steven, 4, 20, 28–29, 31–32, 33, 37, 77, 79, 89, 100, 103
Marxists, 4, 22–23, 25, 38
Masson, Jeffrey, 1, 7, 14, 23, 112
Maxim of Manner, 52
Maxim of Quality, 52, 118, 119
Maxim of Quantity, 51–52, 119
Maxim of Relevance, 52, 119
Maxims of Conversation, 51–54, 118–119
Meaning, 26
Medical analogy, of Freud, 6–7
Memory, 12
Messages, multiple, 49–50
Metalanguage, 62
Methods for discouraging exploitation, 132–135
"Milieu" therapy, 31
Miller, Jean Baker, 130*n*1
Millett, Kate, 130*n*1
Mitchell, Juliet, 38, 112
Moi, Toril, 35, 37
Morality, 107, 130*n*2
Moss, Donald, 59*n*2
Mother of Dora
and the case history summary, 15, 16, 17, 18, 19
and cultural critics, 28
Freud's omissions about, 126, 127–128
and homosexuality, 27, 28

and the interpersonal framework,
   101–110
and possible outcomes for Dora,
   108–109
and transference/countertransfer-
   ence, 27
Mothers, as major force affecting children, 112
Multiple function, principle of, 59n3
Multiple messages, 49–50
Muslim, Hyman, 26–27
Mutual pretense, 100–101
Myths, 67, 75

Neurosis/neurotics, 23, 65, 89
Neutrality, analytic, 74, 88–89, 107,
   97n. See also Objectivity
Normality, 116–117, 122–123, 124,
   130n2

O'Barr, William M., 116
Objectivity, 94–96. See also Neutral-
   ity, analytic
Object relations theory, 23
Oedipus complex, 8, 9, 23–24, 30, 65,
   67–68, 112–114
Omer, Haim, 67
Orthodox analytic theory, 22, 24
Overdetermination, 72, 41–42n2,
   59n3

Passivity, 47–48, 58–59n2
Patients, voluntary, 109–110
Penis envy, 9, 113, 130–131n3
Phallus, 23–24
Phrenology, 9
Pletsch, Carl, 31, 32, 33
Politeness theory, 11, 50–51, 53–54,
   56, 57–58, 61
Political perspective, 34–35, 119–120
Popper, Karl, 34
Postmodernism, 45, 79
Pragmatics, and therapeutic discourse,
   60, 61, 62, 63–65, 75n1
Pragmatic theories/theorists, 4, 11–13,
   26, 40, 49–50, 56–58, 59n3, 98n3
Principle of multiple function, 59n3
Private discourse, 93–94
Prurience, 124–125, 131n6
Psyche, 23, 24, 66, 72, 99, 124, 127

Psychoanalysis
   aims/goals of, 26, 40, 56–57, 66, 70,
      74, 120, 134
   candidates for, 100
   and change, 116–117
   criticisms of, 8–9
   effects of, 5–6
   as a form of interpretation, 121
   as male dominated, 131n5
   as a method of choice, 6
   as a science, 79–80, 123–124
   similarities between linguistics and,
      44–45
   traditional methods of, 10–11
Public discourse, 93–94

Ramas, Maria, 35, 37
"Rat Man," 86–87, 126
Reciprocity/nonreciprocity, 68, 71,
   75–76n4
Reconstruction, 62
Religion. See Theology
Repression, 66
Ricoeur, Paul, 13
Rieff, Philip, 12, 31
Riviere, Joan, 12
Rohrbaugh, Joanna B., 130n1
Roiphe, Herman, 130–131n3
Rose, ZZ, 35

Sachner, Mark, 35
Schafer, Roy, 13, 64, 89, 75n1, 130n1,
   130–131n3
Schismatic analysts, 4
Schofield, William, 14n2
Science/scientific method
   and art, 33, 34, 45
   as authority, 123, 124
   and criticisms of psychoanalysis,
      8–9
   and gender issues, 124
   misunderstanding of, 95–96
   and normality, 123
   and the philosophy of language, 51
   psychoanalysis as a, 79–80, 123–124
   and religion, 10
   as repressive, 9
   and similarities between psychoanal-
      ysis and linguistics, 44–45
Scientific discourse, 93

Scientific document(s)
  case histories as, 31, 32, 33, 34, 78
  characteristics of, 93–95
  *Dora* as a, 78, 79–80, 93–95, 130
Seduction theory, 23
Self-identity, 23–24
Semantics, 26, 37, 40, 48–49, 60–63,
  64, 71, 75*n*1
Sexual matters, 16–17, 18, 24, 73–74,
  113–114, 119–120, 122, 124–
  125, 129
Shapiro, David, 98*n*4
Sincerity, 59*n*3
Singer, Barton, 67
Singer, Margaret T., 58*n*1
Skoller, Eleanor H., 35
Sluzki, Carlos, 106
Social criticism, 22–23, 26, 34–35, 39.
  *See also* Interpersonal systems
  theory
Sociolinguists, 98*n*3
Speech act theory, 50–51, 54–55, 56
Spence, Donald, 34, 92–93, 95–96
Sprengnether, Madelon, 35, 37
Stadlen, Anthony, 76*n*5
Stierlin, Helm, 39
Strachey, Alix, 11–12
Strachey, James, 11–12, 41*n*2
Strauss, Anselm L., 100
*Studies on Hysteria* (Freud), 86–87, 115
Style, of therapist/client, 49–50, 61,
  134–135
Sublimation, 28, 113
Suicide, 20, 106, 119, 120
Symptoms, 1, 23, 74, 99, 105–106,
  118, 119, 120, 121, 131*n*6
Synonymy, 48, 59*n*3
Syntax, 46–47, 48, 60, 62, 63, 59*n*2
Szasz, Thomas, 132

Tannen, Deborah, 116
Teller, Virginia, 59*n*2
Theology, 10, 123, 124
Therapeutic discourse
  and an adversarial model, 81–82, 84
  benefits of, 61–62
  and direct discourse, 82–83, 87
  goals of, 61
  intrapsychic therapy, 74
  and learning language, 70–71

and methods for discouraging exploitation, 134–135
as narrative, 89
and power, 71, 72–73
and pragmatics, 60, 61, 62, 63–65
and prejudice, 85–87
and private/public discourse, 93
and reciprocity/nonreciprocity, 68
and responsibility for intentions in
  communication, 69–70
roles of, 76*n*6
rules of, 73
and semantics, 60–61, 62–63
and social situation, 74
as a special kind of discourse, 62
and syntax, 62, 63
and women, 87–88
Therapist(s)
  and group therapy, 25
  mood/personality of, 12
  and sexual relations between thera-
    pist and patient, 73–74
  training of, 134
  women as, 131*n*5
Thompson, Clara, 24
Tookey, Margaret L., 58*n*1
Transference/countertransference
  and analytic neutrality, 88
  and cultural critics, 28–29
  and the failure of Dora's analysis,
    11, 129–130
  and feminists, 26
  and Freud as an agent for Dora's fa-
    ther, 126, 127
  and Freud's bias against women, 88
  importance of understanding, 3
  and interpersonal problems between
    Freud and Dora, 11, 77–78
  and the Lacanians, 24
  and language, 61, 63
  and literary critics, 28–29
  maternal/paternal, 27, 28
  and methods for discouraging exploi-
    tation, 134
  need for, 9
  and power, 6
  and pragmatic theorists, 40
  and sexual matters, 113–114
Trujillo, Manuel, 59*n*2
Trust, 66–67, 88–89

Truth
  and case histories, 33
  and forms of discourse, 76*n*6
  genetic, 30, 74, 108
  historical, 30, 74, 91, 92, 108
  and life stories, 90
  and the Maxim of Quality, 118
  and speech act theory, 54–55
*Tu quoque* structure, 106–107

Unconscious, 3, 23
Unconventional sentimentality, 74–75

Values, and interpretation, 11
Van Dijk, Teun A., 89
Victimization, 39, 76*n*5, 131*n*6

Waelder, Robert, 59*n*3
Wallerstein, Robert S., 135*n*1
Watzlawick, Paul, 5, 59*n*3
Weakland, John, 5
Weiss-Sampson mastery-control
  model, 75–76*n*4
White, William Alanson, 24
Widiger, Thomas, 100
"Wolf Man," 86, 87, 126
Women. *See* Feminine psychology;
  Feminists; Gender issues
Wynne, Lyman C., 58*n*1

Yalom, Irvin D., 10

Zetzel, E., 63

# About the Authors

**Robin Tolmach Lakoff** is Professor of Linguistics at the University of California at Berkeley. She is the author of *Abstract Syntax and Latin Complementation* (1968), *Language and Woman's Place* (1975), *Talking Power* (1990), and co-author with Raquel Scherr of *Face Value* (1984) and with Mandy Aftel of *When Talk is not Cheap* (1985).

**James C. Coyne** is Professor of Psychology in the Departments of Psychiatry and Family Practice at the University of Michigan Medical School. He is the editor of *Essential Papers on Depression* (1985).